Mediterranean Diet Cookbook for Beginners

2000 Days of Quick & Easy Recipes – No-Stress Delights with a 30-Day Meal Plan & Simple Ingredients for Everyday Cooking

Savoring Healthy Living Without Compromising Taste

Julianna Wiggins

Legal & Disclaimer

The content and information contained in this book has been compiled from reliable sources, which are accurate based on the knowledge, belief, expertise and information of the Author. The author cannot be held liable for any omissions and/or errors.

TABLE OF CONTENTS

INTRODUCTION

Dear readers,

Julianna Wiggins as a professional chef and an expert in the realm of healthy eating, specializes in the art of Mediterranean cuisine. Her profound passion for this culinary style, combined with an in-depth understanding of its health benefits, positions Julianna as an authoritative figure in the world of health-conscious cooking.

Julianna's recipes are a symphony of flavors, colors, and textures, meticulously crafted to promote wellness without sacrificing taste. She appreciates the balance of enjoying food while adhering to a healthy diet, and this enthusiasm resonates throughout her work.

Her journey in mastering Mediterranean cuisine and healthy eating is both professional and personal. Julianna understands the intricacies and challenges that come with adopting a new way of eating and living. Her own transformative experiences fuel her desire to inspire and assist others on their path to wellness.

Julianna has authored this book with the conviction that her knowledge and experience can be life-altering. She is dedicated to providing readers with the necessary tools and insights to achieve their health and dietary goals. Her aim is to make the journey towards healthier living not only achievable but also delightful and rich in flavor.

With Julianna Wiggins as your guide, your exploration into healthy eating and Mediterranean cuisine will be more than just manageable; it will be an adventure filled with taste, health, and joy. Let her lead you to uncover the endless possibilities in the world of healthful, delicious eating.

CHAPTER 1: INTRODUCTION TO THE MEDITERRANEAN DIET

The Mediterranean Diet: A Journey to Health

Embarking on the journey of the Mediterranean diet is much more than adopting a new way of eating; it's embracing a lifestyle steeped in rich cultural traditions and a history of balanced, wholesome living. This diet, originating from the Mediterranean basin, is not only renowned for its flavors but also for its numerous health benefits.

At the heart of the Mediterranean diet is an abundance of fresh, whole foods. The emphasis is on vegetables, fruits, whole grains, nuts, and seeds, with olive oil being the primary source of healthy fats. This diet is unique in its approach to protein - focusing on plant-based sources and seafood, with moderate amounts of dairy, poultry, and eggs. Red meat is consumed less frequently, treasured for its flavor rather than a daily staple.

The Mediterranean diet is as much about what you eat as it is about how you eat. It encourages enjoying meals with family and friends, savoring each bite, and embracing the joy of cooking and eating wholesome food. This holistic approach to eating supports not just physical health but also mental and emotional well-being.

Research has consistently shown that the Mediterranean diet can lead to numerous health benefits, including a lower risk of heart disease, stroke, type 2 diabetes, and certain types of cancer. It's also associated with a lower risk of Alzheimer's and Parkinson's diseases and can aid in maintaining a healthy weight.

The Mediterranean diet's focus on whole foods and healthy fats means it's naturally rich in antioxidants and anti-inflammatory compounds. These nutrients are crucial for maintaining overall health, reducing oxidative stress, and preventing chronic diseases.

In this section, we'll explore the key components of the Mediterranean diet, delve into its rich history, and understand why it's not just a diet but a sustainable and enjoyable way of life. Whether you're looking to improve your health or simply want to enjoy delicious and nutritious food, the Mediterranean diet offers a path to both.

Welcome to your journey to health with the Mediterranean diet – a path that's as delightful to the palate as it is beneficial for the body and mind.

The Benefits of Mediterranean Eating

Embarking on the Mediterranean diet unveils a world of profound health benefits, reflecting a harmonious blend of taste and wellness. Rooted in the eating habits of the Mediterranean region, this diet is not just a culinary trend but a time-tested path to improved health.

A Cornucopia of Fruits and Vegetables

Central to the Mediterranean diet is an emphasis on an array of fresh fruits and vegetables. These ingredients aren't just accompaniments but rather the stars of every dish. Loaded with vitamins, minerals, and fiber, they form the nutritional backbone of the diet. The emphasis on whole grains, fruits, and vegetables means a high intake of fiber, which aids in digestion and helps maintain a healthy weight.

Fruits: Berries, apples, oranges, grapes, figs, melons, pears, and peaches.

Vegetables: Spinach, tomatoes, eggplants, bell peppers, onions, kale, carrots, and broccoli.

Additionally, the Mediterranean diet supports a balanced blood sugar level, making it beneficial for individuals with or at risk of developing type 2 diabetes. The combination of fiber-rich foods and healthy fats helps in regulating blood sugar and insulin sensitivity.

Healthy Fats: Olive Oil and Beyond

One of the primary benefits of Mediterranean eating is its positive impact on heart health. Rich in monounsaturated fats from olive oil and omega-3 fatty acids from fish, this diet contributes to lower cholesterol levels and reduced risk of heart disease. The Mediterranean diet breaks the myth of fearing fats. Instead, it celebrates healthy fats, particularly olive oil, used liberally but thoughtfully in cooking and as dressings.

These fats, including those from avocados and nuts, are heart-healthy and satiating.

Another significant advantage is the diet's impact on brain health. Studies have shown that the Mediterranean diet can help slow cognitive decline and reduce the risk of developing Alzheimer's disease. This is attributed to its high levels of antioxidants and healthy fats, which are essential for brain health.

Olive Oil: Use extra virgin olive oil in dressings and cooking.

Nuts and Seeds: Incorporate almonds, chia seeds, walnuts, and sunflower seeds into your diet.

Avocados: Rich in healthy fats, avocados are versatile and can be used in various recipes.

These sources of healthy fats are essential for maintaining heart health and bring a satisfying richness to your meals.

Wholesome Whole Grains

Refined grains take a back seat, while whole grains like quinoa, farro, and whole wheat become staples. These grains are nutrient-rich, providing the body with essential fiber and serving as a fulfilling base for a variety of dishes.

Breads and Pastas: Opt for varieties made from whole wheat or whole grain.
Ancient Grains: barley, quinoa, farro, and bulgur.
Rice: Brown rice or wild rice varieties.

Lean Proteins: A Balanced Approach

The diet leans heavily on fish and poultry as primary protein sources, incorporating them in moderation. Red meat is reserved for occasional consumption. This approach provides essential nutrients while keeping unhealthy fats in check.

Fish Selection: trout, salmon, sardines, and mackerel.

Poultry Choices: skinless chicken or turkey, ideally grilled or baked.

Legumes Variety: Beans, chickpeas, and lentils are excellent choices.

These sources of protein are healthier, with lower unhealthy fat content than red meat, and are packed with vital nutrients.

Moderate Dairy Intake

Cheeses and yogurts, especially those like feta and Greek yogurt, are integral but enjoyed in moderation, contributing to a balanced intake of protein and calcium.

Cheese and Yogurt: Feta, mozzarella, Greek yogurt – in small to moderate amounts.

The Magic of Herbs and Spices

The Mediterranean diet is also known for its anti-inflammatory properties, thanks to the abundance of antioxidants found in its fresh produce and the liberal use of herbs and spices. These anti-inflammatory benefits play a crucial role in reducing the risk of chronic diseases and improving overall well-being. Flavors in the Mediterranean diet come from an extensive use of herbs and spices, reducing the need for salt. These natural flavor enhancers not only add zest to dishes but also bring various health benefits.

Herbs: cilantro, basil, rosemary, thyme, and parsley in your dishes.

Spices: black pepper, nutmeg, cinnamon, and garlic.

The Role of Wine

In line with the Mediterranean lifestyle, wine, especially red, is enjoyed in moderation. Its consumption with meals is seen as beneficial for heart health due to its antioxidant content.

More Than Just Food

The Mediterranean diet is as much about the social and joyful aspects of eating as it is about the food itself. It promotes sharing meals, enjoying the culinary process, and leading an active lifestyle.

This diet isn't a temporary regimen but a sustainable, enjoyable path to lasting health. It's about making informed, delicious choices that benefit both the body and the soul. Let's dive into the flavors and benefits of Mediterranean eating that await you!

Exploring the Regional Contributions to the Mediterranean Diet

The roots of the Mediterranean diet date back thousands of years, intertwining with the histories of ancient civilizations like the Greeks and Romans. It was in these vibrant societies that the diet's foundational elements – olive oil, wine, grains, and fresh produce – first became staples of daily consumption.

1. The Greek Influence: A Legacy of Simplicity and Freshness

In Greece, the Mediterranean diet is a testament to the power of simplicity. Here, the emphasis is on fresh, seasonal ingredients like tomatoes, cucumbers, and olives. Greek cuisine showcases dishes such as the classic Greek salad (Horiatiki), which combines these fresh vegetables with feta cheese and olive oil, and Moussaka, a rich, layered eggplant and meat casserole. The Greek method of cooking is often straightforward yet flavorful, relying on a few quality ingredients to shine.

2. Italian Flavors: A Fusion of Ingredients and Techniques

Italy's contribution to the Mediterranean diet is marked by its use of diverse ingredients and cooking techniques. Italian cuisine is famous for its pasta dishes, made with whole grains and combined with fresh vegetables, herbs, and olive oil. Ingredients like garlic, tomatoes, and basil are staples in Italian kitchens, contributing to the diet's heart-healthy and anti-inflammatory properties. Dishes like Risotto, made with Arborio rice, and Caprese salad, featuring tomatoes, mozzarella, and basil, exemplify the Italian mastery of flavor and nutrition.

3. The Middle Eastern Palette: Rich Spices and Diverse Grains

The Middle Eastern interpretation of the Mediterranean diet adds a palette of rich spices and a variety of grains. Ingredients like bulgur, chickpeas, and lentils are central to dishes like Tabbouleh and Falafel. Spices such as cumin, coriander, and turmeric not only add depth to dishes but also offer health benefits, including anti-inflammatory properties. This region's use of herbs and spices in cooking has significantly influenced the diet's adoption globally, offering flavors that are robust and health-promoting.

4. North African Influence: A Blend of Aromas and Flavors

North Africa's contribution brings a unique blend of aromatic spices and flavors. Couscous, a staple grain in this region, is often served with vegetables and meats, flavored with spices like saffron and cinnamon. Dishes such as Moroccan Tagine, a slow-cooked stew, encapsulate the fusion of sweet and savory flavors, central to this region's culinary identity.

5. Spanish and Portuguese Contributions: Seafood and Simplicity

The Iberian Peninsula, encompassing Spain and Portugal, adds its flair with a focus on seafood and simple, yet robust flavors. The Spanish Paella, a saffron-flavored rice dish combined with seafood or meats, and the Portuguese Bacalhau, a salted cod dish, are iconic examples of how these cultures have influenced the diet.

The Evolution into Modern Times

In the 20th century, the Mediterranean diet gained global recognition for its health benefits, largely due to the landmark Seven Countries Study which highlighted its role in reducing heart disease. Today, it's celebrated not just as a diet but as a sustainable and enjoyable lifestyle, encompassing a balance of flavors, fresh ingredients, and a focus on communal eating.

Current Scientific Perspectives on the Mediterranean Diet's Health Benefits

The Mediterranean Diet has been rigorously analyzed in scientific circles over recent years. This extensive research underscores its role in:

- Minimizing heart disease risks.
- Reducing occurrences of various cancer types.
- Enhancing mental acuity and lowering Alzheimer's disease risks.

Here are some pivotal studies and their findings that underscore the diet's efficacy:

Cardiovascular Health:

The Lyon Diet Heart Study (France, 1999): This groundbreaking study highlighted a staggering **70%** reduction in heart disease risk among participants adhering to a Mediterranean diet rich in alpha-linolenic acid, primarily sourced from olive oil and nuts.

Seguimiento Universidad de Navarra (SUN) Study (Spain, 2018): Showed that individuals following a Mediterranean diet supplemented with extra-virgin olive oil or nuts experienced a **30%** decrease in major cardiovascular events compared to those on a low-fat diet.

Cancer Prevention:

EPIC Study (Europe, 2013): Demonstrated a **40%** reduction in the risk of colorectal cancer among those closely following the Mediterranean diet. Breast cancer risk was lowered by **30%**, and gastric cancer incidence dropped by **20%.**

Cognitive Health and Alzheimer's Prevention:

Neurological Study in Greece (2017): Indicated a **40%** lower risk of Alzheimer's disease among those adhering to the Mediterranean diet, thanks to its rich composition of healthy fats, antioxidants, and vitamins.

Diabetes Management:

Spanish Study on Type 2 Diabetes (2014): Found that people with type 2 diabetes following the Mediterranean diet had **30%** better blood sugar control compared to those on a traditional low-fat diet.

Longevity and Overall Health:

Multi-Country Mediterranean Diet and Longevity Study (2019): Confirmed a **25%** lower rate of mortality and a significant reduction in chronic disease incidence among those who follow the Mediterranean diet.

UNESCO Recognition and Cultural Significance:

In 2010, UNESCO recognized the Mediterranean Diet as an Intangible Cultural Heritage in countries like Italy, Greece, Spain, and Morocco, acknowledging its integral role in cultural identity and sustainable food practices. These studies provide compelling evidence of the Mediterranean Diet's effectiveness in reducing disease risk, enhancing heart health, and promoting longevity. Each piece of research adds to a growing body of scientific support, establishing this diet as a global model for healthy eating.

CHAPTER 2: 30-DAY MEAL PLAN

Day	Breakfast (400 kcal)	Lunch (500 kcal)	Snack (220 kcal)	Dinner (380 kcal)
Day 1	Shakshuka with Tomatoes (400 kcal) - p.17	Pasta with Roasted Tomato and Basil Sauce (480 kcal) - p.31	Panna Cotta with Lavender Syrup (210 kcal) - p.55	Ratatouille in a Skillet with Minimal Olive Oil (450 kcal) - p.58
Day 2	Greek Yogurt with Honey and Nuts (400 kcal) - p.20	Greek Moussaka with Beef and Eggplant (450 kcal) - p.33	Fresh Figs with Goat Cheese and Honey (200 kcal) - p.50	Niçoise Salad with Grilled Tuna and a Few Anchovies (450 kcal) - p.61
Day 3	Protein Smoothie with Spinach and Avocado (400 kcal) - p.19	Chicken and Spinach Lasagna (450 kcal) - p.31	Nut Halva with Honey and Sesame (220 kcal) - p.53	Baked Salmon with Thyme and Lemon (450 kcal) - p.62
Day 4	Polenta with Mushrooms and Parmesan (400 kcal) - p.22	Lamb Pilaf with Tomatoes (500 kcal) - p.33	Low-Sugar Tiramisu with Whole Grain Biscuits (200 kcal) - p.52	Stuffed Peppers with Quinoa and Low-Fat Feta (450 kcal) - p.4
Day 5	Cottage Cheese Bake with Berries and Nuts (400 kcal) - p.23	Mediterranean Fish Soup with Tomatoes and Dill (500 kcal) - p.36	Baked Sweet Potato Chips with Greek Yogurt (220 kcal) - p.49	Orecchiette with Broccoli, Garlic, and Olive Oil, Whole Wheat Pasta (450 kcal) - p.62
Day 6	Couscous with Vegetables and Green Onions (400 kcal) - p.21	Chicken Bolognese Pasta with Basil (500 kcal) - p.32	Pie with Figs and Almonds (210 kcal) - p.57	Mediterranean Roasted Vegetable Salad with Low-Fat Feta, Pine Nuts (450 kcal) - p.60
Day 7	Whole Grain Pancakes with Fruit Sauce (400 kcal) - p.24	Beef Strudel with Vegetables (480 kcal) - p.34	Bruschetta with Tomatoes, Basil, and Mozzarella (220 kcal) - p.47	Pasta with Basil Pesto and Pine Nuts, Whole Wheat (450 kcal) - p.63
Day 8	Quinoa Salad with Avocado and Citrus (400 kcal) - p.25	Lentil Soup with Curry and Spinach (450 kcal) - p.35	Tartlets with Caramelized Onion and Brie Cheese (210 kcal) - p.47	Whole Grain Mini Pizza with Low-Fat Mozzarella and Tomatoes (450 kcal) - p.63
Day 9	Turkish Menemen with Vegetables (400 kcal) - p.28	Braised Chicken with Olives, Lemon, and Roasted Vegetables (450 kcal) - p.37	Falafel with Tahini Sauce (220 kcal) - p.48	Avocado and Orange Citrus Salad with Mint Dressing (450 kcal) - p.61

Day	Breakfast (400 kcal)	Lunch (500 kcal)	Snack (220 kcal)	Dinner (380 kcal)
Day 10	Focaccia with Tomatoes and Olive Oil (400 kcal) - p.26	Turkish Lamb Kebabs with Mixed Grilled Vegetables (450 kcal) - p.38	Orange Phyllo Tartlets with Honey (210 kcal) - p.56	Baked Mackerel with Lemon and Olives (350 kcal) - p.69
Day 11	Muesli with Seasonal Fruits and Nuts (400 kcal) - p.20	Beef Meatballs in Herbed Tomato Sauce with Steamed Broccoli (490 kcal) - p.37	Eggplant Rolls with Cheese and Tomatoes (210 kcal) - p.49	Braised Cod with Olives and Capers (350 kcal) - p.65
Day 12	Fruit Salad with Mint and Yogurt (400 kcal) - p.22	Braised Pork with Apples, Celery, and Carrots (450 kcal) - p.38	Yogurt Popsicles with Berries and Honey (200 kcal) - p.75	Seafood Paella with Saffron, More Seafood, Less Rice (380 kcal) - p.65
Day 13	Waffles with Figs (400 kcal) - p.27	Chicken Kebab with Yogurt Marinade and Vegetable Skewers (450 kcal) - p.39	Olive Tapenade with Whole Grain Bread (200 kcal) - p.45	Risotto with Sea Scallops and Green Peas (380 kcal) - p.66
Day 14	Chocolate-Banana Pancakes (400 kcal) - p.27	Beef Stew with Mixed Vegetables in Provencal Herbs (450 kcal) - p.39	Olive Oil Cake with Lemon Glaze (220 kcal) - p.55	Grilled Dorado with Vegetables and Herbs, Light Dressing (350 kcal) - p.66
Day 15	Caprese Salad with Mozzarella and Tomatoes (400 kcal) - p.30	Chicken Rollatini with Feta, Spinach, and Roasted Peppers (450 kcal) - p.40	Fresh Berry Sorbet (200 kcal) - p.50	Sea Bass in Foil with Lemon and Rosemary, No Butter (360 kcal) - p.67
Day 16	Pumpkin Pancakes with Nuts and Honey (400 kcal) - p.21	Grilled Chicken with Capers, Lemon Sauce, and a Side of Asparagus 450 kcal) - p.40	Apple Charlotte with Cinnamon (220 kcal) - p.51	Squid Stuffed with Vegetables and Wild Rice (380 kcal) - p.67
Day 17	Kefir Smoothie with Berries and Mint (400 kcal) - p.19	Lamb Patties with Mint Sauce and a Greek Salad (500 kcal) - p.41	Ricotta Cream with Berries and Honey (200 kcal) - p.51	Baked Mussels with Parmesan and Garlic (350 kcal) - p.68
Day 18	Ciabatta with Tomatoes and Basil (400 kcal) - p.26	Beef Goulash with Paprika, Tomatoes, and Green Beans (370 kcal) - p.41	Almond Cookies with Citrus Zest (200 kcal) - p.52	Tuna Steak with Tomato Salsa (380 kcal) - p.68
Day 19	Omelette with Feta and Spinach (400 kcal) - p.18	Baked Chicken Thighs with Mediterranean Vegetables (450 kcal) - p.42	Avocado-Based Chocolate Mousse (210 kcal) - p.53	Shrimp with Grilled Vegetables and Citrus Sauce, More Veggies (350 kcal) - p.69

Day	Breakfast (400 kcal)	Lunch (500 kcal)	Snack (220 kcal)	Dinner (380 kcal)
Day 20	Poached Eggs with Green Salad and Avocado (400 kcal) - p.18	Chicken with Artichokes, Wine Sauce, and Sauteed Spinach (450 kcal) - p.42	Panna Cotta with Lavender Syrup (210 kcal) - p.55	Fish Patties with Herbs and Lemon Aioli (380 kcal) - p.70
Day 21	Couscous with Vegetables and Green Onions 400 kcal) - p.21	Lamb Ribs with Grilled Zucchini (500 kcal) - p.43	Mango and Coconut Milk Mousse (200 kcal) - p.57	Branzino with Tomatoes and Capers in White Wine, Light Sauce (350 kcal) - p.70
Day 22	Whole Grain Pancakes with Fruit Sauce (400 kcal) - p.24	Beef Vegetable Ragout with Herbs and a Quinoa Salad (500 kcal) - p.43	Lemon Curd with Berries (190 kcal) - p.54	Pasta with Shrimp and Garlic Sauce, Whole Wheat, Light on Oil (380 kcal) - p.71
Day 23	Scrambled Eggs with Artichokes and Olives (400 kcal) - p.17	Grilled Chicken Fillet with a Tomato-Cucumber Salad (450 kcal) - p.44	Olive Oil Cake with Lemon Glaze (220 kcal) - p.55	Braised Perch with Vegetables in Tomato Sauce (350 kcal) - p.71
Day 24	Kefir Smoothie with Berries and Mint (400 kcal) - p.19	Pork in Honey-Mustard Marinade with a Side of Grilled Eggplant (450 kcal) - p.44	Eggplant Caviar with Garlic and Herbs (220 kcal) - p.46	Pasta Primavera with Seasonal Vegetables, Whole Wheat Pasta (450 kcal) - p.59
Day 25	Greek Yogurt with Honey and Nuts (400 kcal) - p.20	Fargo Soup with Mushrooms and Fresh Greens (480 kcal) - p.35	Feta Cheese Marinated with Olive Oil and Herbs (200 kcal) - p.46	Warm Quinoa Salad with Grilled Eggplant and Sun-Dried Tomatoes (450 kcal) - p.61
Day 26	Chocolate-Banana Pancakes (400 kcal) - p.27	Mediterranean Fish Soup with Tomatoes and Dill (500 kcal) - p.36	Falafel with Tahini Sauce (220 kcal) - p.48	Baked Salmon with Thyme and Lemon (450 kcal) - p.62
Day 27	Poached Eggs with Green Salad and Avocado (400 kcal) - p.18	Gazpacho with Cucumbers, Tomatoes, and Sweet Peppers (460 kcal) - p.36	Whole Grain Crackers with Avocado and Tomato Salsa (200 kcal) - p.48	Orecchiette with Broccoli, Garlic, and Olive Oil, Whole Wheat Pasta (450 kcal) - p.62
Day 28	Fruit Salad with Mint and Yogurt (400 kcal) - p.22	Braised Chicken with Olives, Lemon, and Roasted Vegetables (450 kcal) - p.37	Tartlets with Caramelized Onion and Brie Cheese (210 kcal) - p.47	Stuffed Peppers with Quinoa and Low-Fat Feta (450 kcal) - p.64

Day	Breakfast (400 kcal)	Lunch (500 kcal)	Snack (220 kcal)	Dinner (380 kcal)
Day 29	Waffles with Figs (400 kcal) - p.27	Beef Meatballs in Herbed Tomato Sauce with Steamed Broccoli (490 kcal) - p.37	Yogurt Popsicles with Berries and Honey (200 kcal) - p.75	Lemon-Herb Calamari Rings with Yogurt Dip (370 kcal) - p.64
Day 30	Turkish Menemen with Vegetables (400 kcal) - p.28	Turkish Lamb Kebabs with Mixed Grilled Vegetables (450 kcal) - p.38	Mango and Coconut Milk Mousse (200 kcal) - p.57	Avocado and Orange Citrus Salad with Mint Dressing (450 kcal) - p.61

Note: We wish to remind you that the 30-Day Meal Plan provided in this book is intended as a guide and a source of inspiration. The caloric content of the dishes is approximate and may vary depending on the portion sizes and specific ingredients. Our meal plan is designed to provide a diverse and balanced menu, rich in proteins, healthy fats, and carbohydrates. This allows you to maintain a healthy eating without sacrificing the joy of enjoying delicious meals every day.

If you find that the calories in the recipes do not completely align with your personal needs or the plan, feel free to adjust the portion sizes. Increase or decrease them to ensure that the meal plan suits your individual goals and preferences. Be creative and enjoy each dish according to your needs!

CHAPTER 3: BREAKFASTS: Delicious Omelets and Frittatas

Scrambled Eggs with Artichokes and Olives

Prep: 10 minutes | Cook: 5 minutes | Serves: 2

Ingredients:

- 4 large eggs (200g)
- 1/2 cup canned artichoke hearts, drained and chopped (120g)
- 1/4 cup pitted Kalamata olives, sliced (40g)
- 2 tbsp olive oil (30ml)
- 1 tbsp grated Parmesan cheese (5g)
- Salt and pepper to taste

Instructions:

1. In a bowl, beat the eggs with salt and pepper.
2. Heat olive oil in a skillet. Add artichokes and olives, sauté for 2 minutes.
3. Pour the eggs into the skillet and cook, stirring gently, until they are set but still soft.
4. Sprinkle with Parmesan cheese and serve.

Nutritional Facts (Per Serving): Calories: 400 | Sugars: 2g | Fat: 28g | Carbohydrates: 12g | Protein: 24g | Fiber: 5g | Sodium: 400mg

Shakshuka with Tomatoes

Prep: 15 minutes | Cook: 20 minutes | Serves: 2

Ingredients:

- 1 can (14 oz or 400g) diced tomatoes
- 4 large eggs (200g)
- 1 small onion, diced (70g)
- 1 bell pepper, diced (120g)
- 2 cloves garlic, minced (6g)
- 2 tbsp olive oil (30ml)
- 1 tsp cumin (2g)
- 1 tsp paprika (2g)
- 1/2 tsp chili powder (1g)
- Fresh cilantro and parsley, chopped (for garnish)
- Salt and pepper to taste

Instructions:

1. Heat olive oil in a skillet. Add onion, bell pepper, and garlic; cook until soft.
2. Stir in tomatoes, cumin, paprika, chili powder, salt, and pepper. Simmer for 10 minutes.
3. Make four wells in the tomato mixture and crack an egg into each.
4. Cover and cook until eggs are set to your liking.
5. Garnish with fresh cilantro and parsley.

Nutritional Facts (Per Serving): Calories: 400 | Sugars: 10g | Fat: 22g | Carbohydrates: 35g | Protein: 18g | Fiber: 8g | Sodium: 500mg

Omelette with Feta and Spinach

Prep: 5 minutes | Cook: 10 minutes | Serves: 1

Ingredients:

- 3 large eggs (150g)
- 1/2 cup fresh spinach, chopped (30g)
- 1/4 cup feta cheese, crumbled (50g)
- 1 tbsp olive oil (15ml)
- Salt and pepper to taste

Instructions:

1. In a bowl, whisk together eggs, salt, and pepper.
2. Heat olive oil in a skillet. Add spinach and sauté until wilted.
3. Pour the eggs over the spinach. Sprinkle feta cheese on top.
4. Cook until the eggs are set, fold the omelette in half, and serve.

Nutritional Facts (Per Serving): Calories: 400 | Sugars: 3g | Fat: 28g | Carbohydrates: 6g | Protein: 30g | Fiber: 2g | Sodium: 700mg

Poached Eggs with Green Salad and Avocado

Prep: 10 minutes | Cook: 5 minutes | Serves: 1

Ingredients:

- 2 large eggs (100g)
- 2 cups mixed greens (spinach, arugula) (60g)
- 1/2 ripe avocado, sliced (100g)
- 1 tbsp olive oil (15ml)
- 1 tsp lemon juice (5ml)
- Salt and pepper to taste

Instructions:

1. Boil water in a pot, reduce to a simmer, and gently poach the eggs for about 4 minutes.
2. Toss mixed greens with olive oil, lemon juice, salt, and pepper.
3. Place salad on a plate, top with sliced avocado and poached eggs.

Nutritional Facts (Per Serving): Calories: 400 | Sugars: 2g | Fat: 30g | Carbohydrates: 15g | Protein: 18g | Fiber: 6g | Sodium: 200mg

CHAPTER 4: BREAKFASTS: Nutrient-Packed Smoothies and Juices

Kefir Smoothie with Berries and Mint

Prep: 5 minutes | Cook: 0 minutes | Serves: 1

Ingredients:

- 1 cup plain kefir (245g)
- 1 cup mixed berries (strawberries, blueberries) (150g)
- 1/2 banana (60g)
- 5 mint leaves (2g)
- 1 tbsp honey (15ml)
- Ice cubes

Instructions:

1. Blend kefir, mixed berries, banana, mint leaves, honey, and ice cubes until smooth.

Nutritional Facts (Per Serving): Calories: 400 | Sugars: 25g | Fat: 8g | Carbohydrates: 70g | Protein: 15g | Fiber: 5g | Sodium: 100mg

Protein Smoothie with Spinach and Avocado

Prep: 5 minutes | Cook: 0 minutes | Serves: 1

Ingredients:

- 1 scoop protein powder (30g)
- 1 cup fresh spinach (30g)
- 1/2 ripe avocado (100g)
- 1/2 banana (60g)
- 1 cup almond milk (240ml)
- Ice cubes

Instructions:

1. Blend protein powder, spinach, avocado, banana, almond milk, and ice cubes until smooth.

Nutritional Facts (Per Serving): Calories: 400 | Sugars: 12g | Fat: 22g | Carbohydrates: 35g | Protein: 20g | Fiber: 8g | Sodium: 150mg

CHAPTER 5: BREAKFASTS: Wholesome Grain and Yogurt Bowls

Greek Yogurt with Honey and Nuts

Prep: 5 minutes | Cook: 0 minutes | Serves: 1

Ingredients:

- 1 cup Greek yogurt (245g)
- 2 tbsp honey (30ml)
- 1/4 cup mixed nuts (almonds, walnuts) (30g)
- A pinch of cinnamon

Instructions:

1. In a bowl, combine Greek yogurt with honey and a pinch of cinnamon.
2. Sprinkle with mixed nuts on top.

Nutritional Facts (Per Serving): Calories: 400 | Sugars: 20g | Fat: 18g | Carbohydrates: 45g | Protein: 20g | Fiber: 3g | Sodium: 60mg

Muesli with Seasonal Fruits and Nuts

Prep: 10 minutes | Cook: 0 minutes | Serves: 1

Ingredients:

- 1/2 cup muesli (60g)
- 1/2 cup almond milk (120ml)
- 1/4 cup chopped seasonal fruits (strawberries, blueberries, apples) (50g)
- 1 tbsp chia seeds (15g)
- 1 tbsp chopped nuts (almonds, walnuts) (15g)

Instructions:

1. Mix muesli with almond milk in a bowl and let it sit for 5 minutes.
2. Top with chopped fruits, chia seeds, and nuts.

Nutritional Facts (Per Serving): Calories: 400 | Sugars: 25g | Fat: 15g | Carbohydrates: 55g | Protein: 10g | Fiber: 7g | Sodium: 30mg

Couscous with Vegetables and Green Onions

Prep: 15 minutes | Cook: 10 minutes | Serves: 2

Ingredients:

- 1 cup couscous (180g)
- 1 cup vegetable broth (240ml)
- 1/2 cup diced bell pepper (75g)
- 1 carrot, diced (60g)
- 1/2 cup frozen peas (70g)
- 1/2 cup diced zucchini (75g)
- 1/4 cup green onions, chopped (25g)
- 1 tbsp olive oil (15ml)
- Salt and pepper to taste

Instructions:

1. Bring vegetable broth to a boil, stir in couscous, cover, and remove from heat. Let it sit for 5 minutes.
2. Heat olive oil in a skillet over medium heat. Sauté zucchini, bell pepper, and carrot until softened, about 5-7 minutes.
3. Stir in peas and cook for another 2 minutes.
4. Fluff the couscous with a fork, then mix in the sautéed vegetables and green onions. Season with salt and pepper.
5. Garnish with green onions and fresh parsley before serving.

Nutritional Facts (Per Serving): Calories: 400 | Sugars: 5g | Fat: 6g | Carbohydrates: 75g | Protein: 15g | Fiber: 8g | Sodium: 300mg

Pumpkin Pancakes with Nuts and Honey

Prep: 15 minutes | Cook: 15 minutes | Serves: 2

Ingredients:

- 1 cup all-purpose flour (120g)
- 1/2 cup pumpkin puree (115g)
- 3/4 cup milk (180ml)
- 1 egg
- 2 tbsp brown sugar (30g)
- 1 tsp baking powder (5g)
- 1/2 tsp cinnamon (1g)
- 1/4 tsp nutmeg (0.5g)
- 1/4 cup chopped nuts (walnuts or pecans) (30g)
- 2 tbsp honey (30ml)
- Butter for cooking

Instructions:

1. Mix flour, baking powder, cinnamon, nutmeg, and brown sugar in a bowl.
2. In another bowl, whisk together pumpkin puree, milk, and egg.
3. Combine the wet and dry ingredients, mix until smooth.
4. Heat a pan with a little butter. Pour batter to form pancakes and cook until bubbles form, then flip.
5. Serve pancakes topped with chopped nuts and drizzled with honey.

Nutritional Facts (Per Serving): Calories: 400 | Sugars: 20g | Fat: 15g | Carbohydrates: 55g | Protein: 10g | Fiber: 3g | Sodium: 300mg

Fruit Salad with Mint and Yogurt

Prep: 10 minutes | Cook: 0 minutes | Serves: 2

Ingredients:

- 1 cup strawberries, halved (150g)
- 1/2 cup blueberries (75g)
- 1 kiwi, peeled and sliced (70g)
- 1 orange, segmented (130g)
- 1/2 cup Greek yogurt (120g)
- 1 tbsp honey (15ml)
- 1 tbsp fresh mint, chopped (1.5g)
- 2 tbsp chopped nuts (almonds, walnuts) (15g)

Instructions:

1. In a bowl, combine the chopped fruits.
2. Mix Greek yogurt with honey and mint, then pour over the fruit.
3. Sprinkle with chopped nuts.

Nutritional Facts (Per Serving): Calories: 400 | Sugars: 25g | Fat: 15g | Carbohydrates: 55g | Protein: 10g | Fiber: 5g | Sodium: 50mg

Polenta with Mushrooms and Parmesan

Prep: 5 minutes | Cook: 20 minutes | Serves: 2

Ingredients:

- 1/2 cup polenta (cornmeal) (70g)
- 2 cups water (480ml)
- 1/2 cup grated Parmesan cheese (50g)
- 1 cup mushrooms, sliced (70g)
- 1 tbsp olive oil (15ml)
- Salt and pepper to taste
- Fresh herbs (parsley, thyme), chopped for garnish (1.5g)

Instructions:

1. Bring water to a boil, gradually whisk in polenta. Reduce heat and simmer, stirring frequently, until thickened.
2. Sauté mushrooms in olive oil until tender.
3. Stir Parmesan cheese into the polenta. Season with salt and pepper.
4. Serve polenta topped with sautéed mushrooms and garnished with parsley.

Nutritional Facts (Per Serving): Calories: 400 | Sugars: 2g | Fat: 15g | Carbohydrates: 50g | Protein: 15g | Fiber: 4g | Sodium: 500mg

Yogurt Parfait with Granola and Fresh Fruits

Prep: 10 minutes | Cook: 0 minutes | Serves: 1

Ingredients:

- 1/2 cup mixed fresh fruits (strawberries, blueberries, kiwi) (75g)
- 1 cup Greek yogurt (245g)
- 1/2 cup granola (40g)
- 1 tbsp honey (15ml)

Instructions:

1. Layer half of the Greek yogurt in a glass.
2. Add a layer of granola, then a layer of mixed fruits.
3. Repeat the layers with the remaining yogurt, granola, and fruits.
4. Drizzle honey on top.

Nutritional Facts (Per Serving): Calories: 400 | Sugars: 30g | Fat: 12g | Carbohydrates: 60g | Protein: 20g | Fiber: 4g | Sodium: 50mg

Cottage Cheese Bake with Berries and Nuts

Prep: 15 minutes | Cook: 20 minutes | Serves: 2

Ingredients:

- 1 cup cottage cheese (225g)
- 1 cup mixed berries (strawberries, blueberries, raspberries) (150g)
- 1/4 cup chopped nuts (almonds, walnuts) (30g)
- 2 tbsp maple syrup (30ml)
- 1/2 tsp vanilla extract (2.5ml)

Instructions:

1. Preheat oven to 350°F (175°C).
2. In a baking dish, combine cottage cheese, half of the berries, nuts, maple syrup, and vanilla extract.
3. Bake for 20 minutes or until set.
4. Top with the remaining fresh berries.

Nutritional Facts (Per Serving): Calories: 400 | Sugars: 25g | Fat: 15g | Carbohydrates: 45g | Protein: 20g | Fiber: 4g | Sodium: 400mg

Whole Grain Pancakes with Fruit Sauce

Prep: 15 minutes | Cook: 10 minutes | Serves: 2

Ingredients:

- 1 cup whole wheat flour (120g)
- 1 cup milk (240ml)
- 1 egg
- 1 tbsp honey (15ml)
- 1 tsp baking powder (5g)
- 1/2 tsp cinnamon (1g)
- 1 cup mixed fruit (berries, diced apples) for sauce (150g)
- 1 tbsp maple syrup (15ml)

Instructions:

1. Mix flour, baking powder, and cinnamon in a bowl.
2. In another bowl, whisk milk, egg, and honey. Combine with dry ingredients.
3. Heat a non-stick pan and pour batter to form pancakes. Cook until bubbles form, then flip.
4. For the sauce, heat mixed fruit in a saucepan with maple syrup until softened.
5. Serve pancakes topped with fruit sauce.

Nutritional Facts (Per Serving): Calories: 400 | Sugars: 25g | Fat: 8g | Carbohydrates: 70g | Protein: 15g | Fiber: 8g | Sodium: 300mg

Bulgur Porridge with Fruits and Nuts

Prep: 5 minutes | Cook: 15 minutes | Serves: 2

Ingredients:

- 1/2 cup bulgur (90g)
- 1 1/2 cups water (360ml)
- 1/4 cup chopped mixed nuts (almonds, walnuts) (30g)
- 1/4 cup mixed dried fruits (raisins, apricots) (40g)
- 1 tbsp honey (15ml)
- 1/2 tsp cinnamon (1g)

Instructions:

1. In a saucepan, bring water to a boil and add bulgur. Reduce heat and simmer until tender, about 12-15 minutes.
2. Stir in honey, cinnamon, mixed nuts, and dried fruits.
3. Serve warm.

Nutritional Facts (Per Serving): Calories: 400 | Sugars: 20g | Fat: 10g | Carbohydrates: 70g | Protein: 10g | Fiber: 8g | Sodium: 10mg

Quinoa Salad with Avocado and Citrus

Prep: 10 minutes | Cook: 15 minutes | Serves: 2

Ingredients:

- 1/2 cup quinoa (85g)
- 1 cup water (240ml)
- 1 avocado, diced (150g)
- 1/2 cup orange segments (100g)
- 1/4 cup chopped red onion (40g)
- 2 tbsp olive oil (30ml)
- 1 tbsp lemon juice (15ml)
- Salt and pepper to taste

Instructions:

1. Rinse quinoa under cold water. In a saucepan, combine quinoa and water. Bring to a boil, then simmer until water is absorbed.
2. In a bowl, mix cooked quinoa, avocado, orange segments, and red onion.
3. Whisk together olive oil, lemon juice, salt, and pepper. Drizzle over the salad and toss.

Nutritional Facts (Per Serving): Calories: 400 | Sugars: 5g | Fat: 20g | Carbohydrates: 50g | Protein: 8g | Fiber: 8g | Sodium: 200mg

Tuna and Vegetable Rolls

Prep: 20 minutes | Cook: 0 minutes | Serves: 2

Ingredients:

- 1 can tuna in water, drained (140g)
- 1/4 cup diced cucumber (40g)
- 1/4 cup shredded carrots (30g)
- 1/4 cup bell pepper, thinly sliced (30g)
- 2 whole grain tortillas (60g each)
- 1 tbsp low-fat greek yogurt (15ml)
- 1 tsp Dijon mustard (5ml)
- Salt and pepper to taste

Instructions:

1. In a bowl, mix tuna, greek yogurt, Dijon mustard, salt, and pepper.
2. Lay tortillas flat and spread the tuna mixture.
3. Add cucumber, carrots, and bell pepper.
4. Roll up tightly and cut into slices.

Nutritional Facts (Per Serving): Calories: 400 | Sugars: 5g | Fat: 15g | Carbohydrates: 40g | Protein: 25g | Fiber: 5g | Sodium: 600mg

Focaccia with Tomatoes and Olive Oil

Prep: 20 minutes + 1 hour rising | Cook: 20 minutes | Serves: 8

Ingredients:

- 2 1/4 cups all-purpose flour (270g)
- 1 tsp instant yeast (3g)
- 1 tsp sugar (4g)
- 1 tsp salt (5g)
- 1 cup warm water (240ml)
- 3 tbsp olive oil, divided (45ml)
- 2 medium tomatoes, thinly sliced (200g)
- 1 tsp dried oregano (1g)
- 1/2 tsp coarse sea salt (2.5g)

Instructions:

1. Mix flour, yeast, sugar, and salt in a large bowl.
2. Add warm water and 1 tablespoon olive oil, and knead until smooth.
3. Cover dough and let rise for 1 hour.
4. Preheat oven to 400°F (200°C). Press dough into a greased baking sheet.
5. Top with tomato slices, drizzle with remaining olive oil, sprinkle with oregano and sea salt.
6. Bake for 20 minutes or until golden.

Nutritional Facts (Per Serving): Calories: 400 | Sugars: 2g | Fat: 10g | Carbohydrates: 68g | Protein: 10g | Fiber: 3g | Sodium: 600mg

Ciabatta with Tomatoes and Basil

Prep: 5 minutes | Cook: 0 minutes | Serves: 2

Ingredients:

- 1 ciabatta loaf, sliced in half (250g)
- 2 medium tomatoes, sliced (200g)
- 1/4 cup fresh basil leaves (15g)
- 2 tbsp olive oil (30ml)
- Salt and pepper to taste

Instructions:

1. Drizzle olive oil over ciabatta halves.
2. Arrange tomato slices and basil leaves on top.
3. Season with salt and pepper.

Nutritional Facts (Per Serving): Calories: 400 | Sugars: 5g | Fat: 14g | Carbohydrates: 60g | Protein: 10g | Fiber: 4g | Sodium: 500mg

Chocolate-Banana Pancakes

Prep: 10 minutes | Cook Time: 15 minutes | Serves: 4

Ingredients:

- 1 1/2 cups all-purpose flour (187.5g)
- 2 tbsp cocoa powder (10g)
- 2 tsp baking powder
- 1 ripe banana, mashed (118g)
- 1 1/4 cups milk (300ml)
- 1 egg (about 50g)
- 2 tbsp melted butter (30ml)
- Chocolate chips (optional, amount varies, typically around 1/4 cup or 45g if used)

Instructions:

1. Combine flour, cocoa powder, and baking powder in a bowl.
2. In another bowl, mix the mashed banana, milk, egg, and melted butter.
3. Stir the wet ingredients into the dry ingredients until just combined. Add chocolate chips if desired.
4. Cook spoonfuls of the batter on a hot, lightly greased griddle or pan, flipping once.
5. Serve with additional banana slices and a drizzle of maple syrup or honey.

Nutritional Information (Per Serving): Calories: 320 | Fat: 10g | Carbohydrates: 50g | Protein: 8g | Fiber: 3g

Waffles with Figs

Prep Time: 15 minutes | Cook Time: 20 minutes | Serves: 4

Ingredients:

- 2 cups all-purpose flour (250g)
- 2 tsp baking powder
- 1/2 tsp salt
- 2 tbsp sugar (25g)
- 2 eggs (100g)
- 1 3/4 cups milk (420ml)
- 1/2 cup unsalted butter, melted (113g)
- 1 tsp vanilla extract (5ml)

For Serving:
- Greek yogurt (amount varies, typically around 1/2 cup or 120g per serving)
- Fresh figs (amount varies, typically 1-2 figs per serving, 40-80g)
- Honey (to taste, usually about 1 tbsp or 15ml per serving)

Instructions:

1. In a large bowl, whisk together flour, baking powder, salt, and sugar.
2. In another bowl, beat the eggs and then mix in the milk, melted butter, and vanilla extract.
3. Pour the wet ingredients into the dry ingredients and stir until just combined.
4. Preheat a waffle iron and lightly grease it.
5. Pour the batter into the waffle iron and cook according to the manufacturer's instructions, usually about 3-5 minutes per waffle.
6. Serve the waffles topped with Greek yogurt, fresh sliced figs, and a drizzle of honey.

Nutritional Information (Per Serving): Calories: 400 | Fat: 20g | Carbohydrates: 48g | Protein: 10g | Fiber: 2g

CHAPTER 6: BREAKFASTS: Quick and Healthy

Turkish Menemen with Vegetables

Prep: 10 minutes | Cook: 20 minutes | Serves: 2

Ingredients:

- 4 large eggs (200g)
- 1 small onion, chopped (70g)
- 1 bell pepper, chopped (120g)
- 2 tomatoes, diced (200g)
- 2 tbsp olive oil (30ml)
- 1 tsp paprika (2g)
- Salt and pepper to taste
- Fresh parsley for garnish (5g)

Instructions:

1. Heat olive oil in a skillet. Add onion and bell pepper, cook until soft.
2. Stir in tomatoes, paprika, salt, and pepper. Cook until tomatoes are soft.
3. Crack eggs over the mixture. Cover and cook until eggs are set to your liking.
4. Garnish with fresh parsley.

Nutritional Facts (Per Serving): Calories: 400 | Sugars: 8g | Fat: 28g | Carbohydrates: 22g | Protein: 18g | Fiber: 4g | Sodium: 500mg

Traditional Greek Salad with Olive Oil

Prep: 10 minutes | Cook: 0 minutes | Serves: 2

Ingredients:

- 2 cups chopped cucumber (300g)
- 2 medium tomatoes, chopped (200g)
- 1/4 cup sliced red onion (40g)
- 1/2 cup feta cheese, crumbled (100g)
- 1/4 cup Kalamata olives (50g)
- 2 tbsp olive oil (30ml)
- 1 tbsp red wine vinegar (15ml)
- 1/2 tsp dried oregano (1g)
- Salt and pepper to taste

Instructions:

1. Combine cucumber, tomatoes, red onion, feta cheese, and olives in a bowl.
2. Whisk together olive oil, red wine vinegar, oregano, salt, and pepper.
3. Pour the dressing over the salad and toss.

Nutritional Facts (Per Serving): Calories: 400 | Sugars: 8g | Fat: 28g | Carbohydrates: 30g | Protein: 10g | Fiber: 5g | Sodium: 800mg

Sun-dried Tomato Hummus Sandwich

Prep Time: 10 minutes | Cook Time: 0 minutes | Serves: 2

Ingredients:

- 1/4 cup sun-dried tomatoes in oil, drained (54g)
- 1 can (15 oz) chickpeas, drained and rinsed (425g)
- 1/4 cup tahini (60ml)
- 2 tbsp olive oil (30ml)
- Juice of 1 lemon (3 tbsp or 45ml)
- 1 clove garlic, minced (3g)
- Salt and pepper to taste
- 4 slices whole grain bread
- Fresh lettuce and sliced cucumber for sandwich filling (lettuce 5g per leaf, cucumber slices 40g total)

Instructions:

1. In a food processor, blend sun-dried tomatoes, chickpeas, tahini, olive oil, lemon juice, garlic, salt, and pepper until smooth.
2. Spread the sun-dried tomato hummus on whole grain bread slices.
3. Add lettuce and cucumber slices to make sandwiches.

Nutritional Information (Per Serving): Calories: 380 | Fat: 20g | Carbohydrates: 42g | Protein: 13g | Fiber: 9g

Hummus with Warm Whole Grain Bread and Vegetables

Prep: 25 minutes | Cook: 0 minutes | Serves: 2

Ingredients:

For Hummus:
- 1 cup canned chickpeas, drained and rinsed (240g)
- 2 tbsp tahini (30ml)
- 2 cloves garlic, minced (6g)
- 2 tbsp lemon juice (30ml)
- 2 tbsp olive oil (30ml), plus more for drizzling
- Salt and pepper to taste
- 1/4 tsp ground cumin (0.5g)
- 1/4 cup water (60ml)

Ingredients for Serving:
- 4 slices whole grain bread, toasted (120g)
- 1/2 cup sliced cucumber (75g)
- 1/2 cup sliced bell peppers (75g)
- 1/4 cup sliced carrots (30g)

Instructions:

1. In a food processor, blend chickpeas, tahini, garlic, lemon juice, 2 tablespoons olive oil, salt, pepper, and cumin until smooth.
2. Gradually add water until desired consistency is reached.
3. Spread the homemade hummus evenly on toasted whole grain bread slices.
4. Arrange sliced cucumber, bell peppers, and carrots on the side. Drizzle additional olive oil over hummus.

Nutritional Facts (Per Serving): Calories: 400 | Sugars: 8g | Fat: 20g | Carbohydrates: 45g | Protein: 15g | Fiber: 10g | Sodium: 600mg

Caprese Salad with Mozzarella and Tomatoes

Prep: 10 minutes | Cook: 0 minutes | Serves: 2

Ingredients:

- 2 medium tomatoes, sliced (200g)
- 8 oz fresh mozzarella cheese, sliced (225g)
- 1/4 cup fresh basil leaves (15g)
- 2 tbsp olive oil (30ml)
- 1 tbsp balsamic vinegar (15ml)
- Salt and pepper to taste

Instructions:

1. Arrange alternating slices of tomato and mozzarella cheese on a plate.
2. Scatter basil leaves over the top.
3. Drizzle with olive oil and balsamic vinegar.
4. Season with salt and pepper.

Nutritional Facts (Per Serving): Calories: 400 | Sugars: 5g | Fat: 30g | Carbohydrates: 10g | Protein: 20g | Fiber: 2g | Sodium: 300mg

Tuna Sandwich with Fresh Vegetables

Prep: 10 minutes | Cook: 0 minutes | Serves: 2

Ingredients:

- 1 can tuna in water, drained (140g)
- 4 slices whole grain bread (120g)
- 1/4 cup low-fat greek yogurt (60ml)
- 1/4 cucumber, thinly sliced (50g)
- 1 small tomato, thinly sliced (50g)
- 1/4 red onion, thinly sliced (25g)
- Lettuce leaves (20g)
- Salt and pepper to taste

Instructions:

1. Mix tuna with greek yogurt, salt, and pepper.
2. Spread the tuna mixture on two bread slices.
3. Top with cucumber, tomato, red onion, and lettuce.
4. Cover with the remaining bread slices.

Nutritional Facts (Per Serving): Calories: 400 | Sugars: 6g | Fat: 15g | Carbohydrates: 40g | Protein: 30g | Fiber: 5g | Sodium: 600mg

Pasta with Roasted Tomato and Basil Sauce

Prep: 15 minutes | Cook: 25 minutes | Serves: 4

Ingredients:

- Whole wheat pasta (2 cups, dry) (200g)
- Cherry tomatoes (2 cups) (300g)
- Fresh basil leaves (1/2 cup) (15g)
- Olive oil (2 tbsp) (30ml)
- Garlic, minced (2 cloves) (6g)
- Balsamic vinegar (1 tbsp) (15ml)
- Salt and pepper to taste

Instructions:

1. Preheat oven to 400°F (200°C). Toss tomatoes with 1 tbsp olive oil, salt, and pepper. Roast for 20 minutes.
2. Cook pasta according to package instructions. Drain and set aside.
3. In a pan, heat remaining olive oil. Add garlic and cook until fragrant.
4. Add roasted tomatoes, balsamic vinegar, and half of the basil. Cook for 5 minutes.
5. Toss pasta with the sauce. Garnish with remaining basil.

Nutritional Facts (Per Serving): Calories: 480 | Sugars: 5g | Fat: 10g | Carbohydrates: 85g | Protein: 15g | Fiber: 8g | Sodium: 5g

Chicken and Spinach Lasagna

Prep: 20 minutes | Cook: 45 minutes | Serves: 6

Ingredients:

- Whole wheat lasagna noodles (9 sheets) (180g)
- Cooked chicken breast, shredded (2 cups) (300g)
- Spinach, chopped (2 cups) (60g)
- Ricotta cheese (1 cup) (250g)
- Mozzarella cheese, shredded (1 cup) (100g)
- Tomato sauce (2 cups) (500ml)
- Garlic powder, onion powder, Italian seasoning (1 tsp each)
- Salt and pepper to taste

Instructions:

1. Preheat oven to 375°F (190°C). Cook lasagna noodles as per package instructions.
2. In a bowl, mix chicken, spinach, ricotta, half mozzarella, and spices.
3. Spread a layer of tomato sauce in a baking dish.
4. Layer noodles, chicken mixture, and sauce. Repeat.

5. Top with remaining mozzarella. Bake for 25-30 minutes until bubbly.

Nutritional Facts (Per Serving): Calories: 450 | Sugars: 6g | Fat: 12g | Carbohydrates: 45g | Protein: 40g | Fiber: 5g | Sodium: 7

Couscous with Braised Lamb and Vegetables

Prep: 20 minutes | Cook: 60 minutes | Serves: 4

Ingredients:

- Couscous (1 cup) (180g)
- Lamb shoulder, cut into cubes (1 lb) (450g)
- Carrots, chopped (1 cup) (130g)
- Zucchini, chopped (1 cup) (120g)
- Onion, diced (1 cup) (160g)
- Garlic cloves, minced (2) (6g)
- Canned diced tomatoes (1 cup) (240ml)
- Chicken broth (2 cups) (480ml)
- Cumin (1 tsp) (2g)
- Coriander (1 tsp) (2g)
- Cinnamon (1/2 tsp) (1g)
- Olive oil (2 tbsp) (30ml)
- Salt and pepper to taste

Instructions:

1. In a large pot, heat olive oil. Add lamb cubes, season with salt and pepper, and brown on all sides. Remove and set aside.
2. In the same pot, add onions, garlic, carrots, and zucchini. Cook until softened.
3. Return lamb to the pot, add cumin, coriander, cinnamon, tomatoes, and chicken broth. Bring to a boil, then reduce heat and simmer for 45 minutes.
4. Prepare couscous according to package instructions.
5. Serve braised lamb and vegetables over couscous.

Nutritional Facts (Per Serving): Calories: 480 | Sugars: 6g | Fat: 15g | Carbohydrates: 50g | Protein: 35g | Fiber: 7g | Sodium: 8g

Chicken Bolognese Pasta with Basil

Prep: 10 minutes | Cook: 30 minutes | Serves: 4

Ingredients:

- Whole wheat spaghetti (2 cups, dry) (200g)
- Ground chicken breast (1 lb) (450g)
- Tomato paste (1/4 cup) (60ml)
- Carrots, diced (1/2 cup) (60g)
- Celery, diced (1/2 cup) (60g)
- Onion, diced (1/2 cup) (80g)
- Garlic, minced (2 cloves) (6g)
- Chicken broth (1 cup) (240ml)
- Fresh basil, chopped (1/4 cup) (10g)
- Olive oil (1 tbsp) (15ml)
- Salt and pepper to taste

Instructions:

1. Cook pasta according to package instructions. Drain and set aside.
2. In a large pan, heat olive oil. Add onions, carrots, celery, and garlic. Cook until soft.
3. Add ground chicken, cook until browned.
4. Stir in tomato paste, chicken broth, salt, and pepper. Simmer for 20 minutes.
5. Toss pasta with the Bolognese sauce. Garnish with fresh basil.

Nutritional Facts (Per Serving): Calories: 500 | Sugars: 7g | Fat: 15g | Carbohydrates: 55g | Protein: 35g | Fiber: 7g | Sodium: 8g

Greek Moussaka with Beef and Eggplant

Prep: 30 minutes | Cook: 60 minutes | Serves: 6

Ingredients:

- Eggplants, sliced (3 medium) (750g)
- Ground beef (1 lb) (450g)
- Onion, chopped (1 cup) (160g)
- Garlic, minced (2 cloves)
- Canned crushed tomatoes (1 cup) (240ml)
- Cinnamon (1 tsp) (2g)
- Cumin (1 tsp) (2g)
- Olive oil (1 tbsp) (15ml)
- Salt and pepper to taste
- Allspice (1/2 tsp) (1g)
- Cinnamon (1/2 tsp) (1g)

Instructions:

1. Salt eggplant slices and set aside for 20 minutes. Rinse and pat dry.

2. In a skillet, heat 1 tbsp olive oil. Cook eggplants until browned. Set aside.

3. In the same skillet, add remaining oil, onion, garlic, and ground beef. Cook until brown.

4. Add tomatoes, allspice, cinnamon, salt, and pepper. Simmer for 15 minutes.

5. For béchamel sauce, melt butter, whisk in flour, and gradually add milk. Cook until thickened.

6. Layer eggplant, meat sauce, and béchamel in a baking dish. Top with Parmesan.

7. Bake at 350°F (175°C) for 40 minutes.

Nutritional Facts (Per Serving): Calories: 450 | Sugars: 8g | Fat: 20g | Carbohydrates: 35g | Protein: 30g | Fiber: 6g | Sodium: 10g

Lamb Pilaf with Tomatoes

Prep: 15 minutes | Cook: 40 minutes | Serves: 4

Ingredients:

- Brown rice (1 cup) (190g)
- Lamb, diced (1 lb) (450g)
- Canned diced tomatoes (1 cup) (240ml)
- Onion, chopped (1 cup) (160g)
- Chicken broth (2 cups) (480ml)
- Juice of 1 lemon (3 tbsp 45ml)
- 1/4 cup olive oil (60ml)
- Salt and pepper to taste

Instructions:

1. In a pot, heat olive oil. Add lamb and brown on all sides. Remove and set aside.

2. In the same pot, add onion. Cook until translucent.

3. Add rice, cumin, cinnamon, and cook for 1-2 minutes.

4. Add tomatoes, chicken broth, lamb, salt, and

pepper. Bring to a boil.

5. Reduce heat, cover, and simmer for 30 minutes until rice is cooked.

Nutritional Facts (Per Serving): Calories: 500 | Sugars: 4g | Fat: 20g | Carbohydrates: 45g | Protein: 35g | Fiber: 4g | Sodium: 10g

Beef Strudel with Vegetables

Prep: 25 minutes | Cook: 30 minutes | Serves: 4

Ingredients:

- Phyllo dough sheets (4) (160g)
- Ground beef (1 lb) (450g)
- Spinach, chopped (1 cup) (30g)
- Red bell pepper, chopped (1/2 cup) (75g)
- Onion, chopped (1/2 cup) (80g)
- Feta cheese, crumbled (1/2 cup) (75g)
- Olive oil (1 tbsp) (15ml)
- Egg, beaten (for glaze) (50g)
- Salt and pepper to taste

Instructions:

1. Preheat oven to 375°F (190°C).
In a skillet, heat oil. Add onion, bell pepper, and cook until soft.
2. Add ground beef, cook until browned. Stir in spinach, remove from heat.
3. Lay out phyllo sheets, brush each with olive oil.
4. Place beef mixture and feta on the sheets.
5. Roll the phyllo around the filling, brush with egg.
6. Bake for 25-30 minutes until golden brown.

Nutritional Facts (Per Serving): Calories: 480 | Sugars: 3g | Fat: 25g | Carbohydrates: 30g | Protein: 35g | Fiber: 3g | Sodium: 15g

Beef Steak with Arugula and Parmesan Salad

Prep: 10 minutes | Cook: 10 minutes | Serves: 2

Ingredients:

- Beef steak (8 oz each) (225g each)
- Arugula (2 cups) (40g)
- Shaved Parmesan cheese (1/4 cup) (25g)
- Cherry tomatoes, halved (1 cup) (150g)
- Balsamic vinegar (2 tbsp) (30ml)
- Olive oil (for steak) (1 tbsp) (15ml)
- Salt and pepper to taste

Instructions:

1. Season steak with salt and pepper. Heat olive oil in a skillet over medium-high heat.
2. Cook steak for 4-5 minutes per side for medium-rare, or to desired doneness.
3. In a bowl, toss arugula, cherry tomatoes, shaved Parmesan, 1 tbsp olive oil, and balsamic vinegar.
4. Let steak rest for 5 minutes, then slice thinly.
5. Serve the steak slices over the arugula salad.

Nutritional Facts (Per Serving): Calories: 490 | Sugars: 4g | Fat: 30g | Carbohydrates: 8g | Protein: 45g | Fiber: 2g | Sodium: 7g

CHAPTER 9: LUNCHES: Heartwarming Soups and Broths

Fargo Soup with Mushrooms and Fresh Greens

Prep: 15 minutes | Cook: 30 minutes | Serves: 4

Ingredients:

- Fargo (1 cup) (200g)
- Mixed mushrooms, sliced (shiitake, cremini) (2 cups) (300g)
- Fresh greens (spinach, kale) (2 cups) (60g)
- Carrots, diced (1/2 cup) (65g)
- Onion, chopped (1 cup) (160g)
- Garlic, minced (2 cloves) (6g)
- Vegetable broth (4 cups) (960ml)
- Olive oil (1 tbsp) (15ml)
- Thyme (1 tsp) (1g)
- Salt and pepper to taste)

Instructions:

1. In a large pot, heat olive oil. Add onions and garlic, sauté until translucent.
2. Add carrots and mushrooms, cook for 5 minutes.
3. Stir in farro, thyme, salt, and pepper. Cook for 2 minutes.
4. Pour in vegetable broth. Bring to a boil, then simmer for 20 minutes.
5. Add fresh greens, cook until wilted.
6. Adjust seasoning to taste.

Nutritional Facts (Per Serving): Calories: 480 | Sugars: 5g | Fat: 8g | Carbohydrates: 85g | Protein: 15g | Fiber: 12g | Sodium: 10g.

Lentil Soup with Curry and Spinach

Prep: 10 minutes | Cook: 25 minutes | Serves: 4

Ingredients:

- Lentils (1 cup) (200g)
- Spinach, chopped (2 cups) (60g)
- Onion, diced (1 cup) (160g)
- Garlic, minced (2 cloves) (6g)
- Carrot, diced (1/2 cup) (65g)
- Curry powder (2 tsp) (4g)
- Vegetable broth (4 cups) (960ml)
- Canned diced tomatoes (1 cup) (240ml)
- Olive oil (1 tbsp) (15ml)
- Salt and pepper to taste

Instructions:

1. In a pot, heat olive oil. Add onion, garlic, and carrot. Sauté until soft.
2. Stir in curry powder and cook for 1 minute.
3. Add lentils, tomatoes, and vegetable broth. Bring to a boil.

4. Reduce heat and simmer for 20 minutes, until lentils are tender.

5. Stir in spinach until wilted. Season with salt and pepper.

Nutritional Facts (Per Serving): Calories: 450 | Sugars: 6g | Fat: 9g | Carbohydrates: 70g | Protein: 20g | Fiber: 15g | Sodium: 10g

Mediterranean Fish Soup with Tomatoes and Dill

Prep: 20 minutes | Cook: 30 minutes | Serves: 4

Ingredients:

- White fish fillets (such as cod) (1 lb) (450g)
- Onion, chopped (1 cup) (160g)
- Garlic, minced (2 cloves) (6g)
- Canned diced tomatoes (2 cups) (480ml)
- Fresh dill, chopped (1/4 cup) (10g)
- Olive oil (1 tbsp) (15ml)
- Lemon juice (2 tbsp) (30ml)
- Salt and pepper to taste
- Fish or vegetable broth (4 cups) (960ml)

Instructions:

1. In a large pot, heat olive oil. Add onion and garlic, cook until soft.

2. Pour in tomatoes and broth. Bring to a simmer. Add fish, simmer for 10 minutes until fish is cooked through.

3. Stir in lemon juice and dill. Season with salt and pepper. Serve hot.

Nutritional Facts (Per Serving): Calories: 500 | Sugars: 6g | Fat: 12g | Carbohydrates: 15g | Protein: 35g | Fiber: 3g | Sodium: 10g to taste.

Gazpacho with Cucumbers, Tomatoes, and Sweet Peppers

Prep: 15 minutes | Cook: 0 minutes (Chill Time: 2 hours) | Serves: 4

Ingredients:

- Cucumbers, peeled and chopped (2 medium) (300g)
- Ripe tomatoes, chopped (4 large) (800g)
- Red sweet peppers, chopped (2) (300g)
- Red onion, chopped (1/2 cup) (80g)
- Garlic clove, minced (1) (3g)
- Red wine vinegar (2 tbsp) (30ml)
- Extra virgin olive oil (2 tbsp) (30ml)
- Cold water (1 cup) (240ml)
- Salt and pepper to taste
- Fresh basil leaves for garnish (optional))

Instructions:

1. In a large bowl, combine cucumbers, tomatoes, sweet peppers, onion, and garlic.

2. Add red wine vinegar, olive oil, salt, and pepper. Mix well.

3. Blend the mixture in batches until smooth. Add cold water to reach desired consistency.

4. Chill in the refrigerator for at least 2 hours.

5. Adjust seasoning if necessary before serving.

6. Serve cold, garnished with fresh basil leaves if desired.

Nutritional Facts (Per Serving): Calories: 460 | Sugars: 15g | Fat: 15g | Carbohydrates: 50g | Protein: 8g | Fiber: 8g | Sodium: 7g

CHAPTER 10: LUNCHES: Protein-Packed Meat and Poultry Recipes

Braised Chicken with Olives, Lemon, and Roasted Vegetables

Prep: 20 minutes | Cook: 40 minutes | Serves: 4

Ingredients:

- Chicken thighs, skinless (4 thighs) (600g)
- Kalamata olives (1/2 cup) (50g)
- Lemon, sliced (1 medium) (100g)
- Assorted vegetables (bell peppers, zucchini) (2 cups) (300g)
- Chicken broth (1 cup) (240ml)
- Olive oil (1 tbsp) (15ml)
- Fresh herbs (thyme, rosemary) (1 tsp) (1g)
- Garlic, minced (2 cloves) (6g)
- Salt and pepper to taste

Instructions:

1. Season chicken with salt, pepper, and herbs.

2. Heat olive oil in a skillet. Brown chicken on both sides, then remove from skillet.
3. In the same skillet, sauté garlic, then add vegetables, lemon slices, and olives.
4. Place chicken back in the skillet, add broth. Bring to a simmer.
5. Cover and cook in the oven at 375°F (190°C) for 30 minutes.

6. Serve the chicken with vegetables and sauce.

Nutritional Facts (Per Serving): Calories: 450 | Sugars: 5g | Fat: 25g | Carbohydrates: 15g | Protein: 40g | Fiber: 4g | Sodium: 8g

Beef Meatballs in Herbed Tomato Sauce with Steamed Broccoli

Prep:15 minutes | Cook: 30 minutes | Serves: 4

Ingredients:

For Meatballs:
- Ground beef (1 lb) (450g)
- Whole wheat breadcrumbs (1/2 cup) (60g)
- Egg (1) (50g)
- Broccoli florets (4 cups) (300g)
- Canned tomato sauce (2 cups) (480ml)

For Tzatziki Sauce:
- Fresh basil, chopped (1 tbsp) (3g)
- Olive oil (1 tbsp) (15ml)
- Garlic powder, onion powder (1 tsp each) (2g each)
- Salt and pepper to taste

Instructions:

1. Mix ground beef, breadcrumbs, egg, garlic powder, onion powder, salt, and pepper.
2. Form into meatballs and brown in olive oil in a skillet.

3. Pour tomato sauce over meatballs, add basil, and simmer for 20 minutes.

4. Steam broccoli until tender.

5. Serve meatballs with tomato sauce and steamed broccoli.

Nutritional Facts (Per Serving): Calories: 490 | Sugars: 6g | Fat: 28g | Carbohydrates: 20g | Protein: 40g | Fiber: 5g | Sodium: 10g

Turkish Lamb Kebabs with Mixed Grilled Vegetables

Prep 30 minutes (plus marinating) | Cook: 10 minutes | Serves: 4

Ingredients:

- Lamb, cubed (1 lb) (450g)
- Assorted vegetables (eggplant, bell peppers, onions) (2 cups) (300g)
- Yogurt (1/2 cup) (120ml)
- Lemon juice (2 tbsp) (30ml)
- Olive oil (2 tbsp) (30ml)
- Paprika, cumin, garlic powder (1 tsp each) (2g each)
- Fresh mint, chopped (1 tbsp) (3g)
- Salt and pepper to taste

Instructions:

1. Marinate lamb in yogurt, lemon juice, olive oil, paprika, cumin, garlic powder, mint, salt, and pepper for at least 2 hours.

2. Thread lamb and vegetables onto skewers.

3. Grill kebabs over medium heat, turning occasionally, until lamb is cooked to desired doneness, about 6-8 minutes.

4. Serve kebabs with additional lemon wedges.

Nutritional Facts (Per Serving): Calories: 450 | Sugars: 6g | Fat: 25g | Carbohydrates: 15g | Protein: 40g | Fiber: 4g | Sodium: 10g

Braised Pork with Apples, Celery, and Carrots

Prep: 20 minutes | Cook: 1 hour 30 minutes | Serves: 4

Ingredients:

- Pork shoulder, trimmed (1 lb) (450g)
- Apples, cored and sliced (2 medium) (300g)
- Celery, chopped (1 cup) (100g)
- Carrots, chopped (1 cup) (130g)
- Onion, chopped (1 cup) (160g)
- Chicken broth (2 cups) (480ml)
- Olive oil (1 tbsp) (15ml)
- Fresh thyme (1 tsp) (1g)
- Salt and pepper to taste

Instructions:

1. Season pork with salt, pepper, and thyme.

2. In a large pot, heat olive oil. Brown pork on all sides. Remove and set aside.

3. In the same pot, add onions, carrots, celery, and cook until softened.

4. Return pork to the pot. Add apples and chicken

broth.

5. Cover and simmer on low heat for 1 hour 30 minutes until pork is tender.

6. Serve the pork with vegetables and broth.

Nutritional Facts (Per Serving): Calories: 450 | Sugars: 10g | Fat: 18g | Carbohydrates: 25g | Protein: 40g | Fiber: 4g | Sodium: 10g

Chicken Kebab with Yogurt Marinade and Vegetable Skewers

Prep: 30 minutes (plus marinating) | Cook: 10 minutes | Serves: 4

Ingredients:

- Chicken breast, cubed (1 lb) (450g)
- Greek yogurt (1/2 cup) (120ml)
- Lemon juice (2 tbsp) (30ml)
- Garlic, minced (1 clove) (3g)
- Cumin, paprika (1 tsp each) (2g each)
- Assorted vegetables (bell peppers, onions, zucchini) (2 cups) (300g)
- Olive oil (1 tbsp) (15ml)
- Salt and pepper to taste

Instructions:

1. Mix yogurt, lemon juice, garlic, cumin, paprika, salt, and pepper for marinade.

2. Add chicken to the marinade, refrigerate for at least 2 hours.

3. Thread marinated chicken and vegetables onto skewers.

4. Grill over medium heat, turning occasionally, until chicken is cooked, about 10 minutes.

5. Serve hot.

Nutritional Facts (Per Serving): Calories: 450 | Sugars: 6g | Fat: 15g | Carbohydrates: 15g | Protein: 55g | Fiber: 4g | Sodium: 10g

Beef Stew with Mixed Vegetables in Provencal Herbs

Prep: 20 minutes | Cook: 2 hours | Serves:4

Ingredients:

- Beef chuck, cubed (1 lb) (450g)
- Mixed vegetables (carrots, potatoes, green beans) (3 cups) (450g)
- Onion, chopped (1 cup) (160g)
- Beef broth (2 cups) (480ml)
- Canned diced tomatoes (1 cup) (240ml)
- Olive oil (1 tbsp) (15ml)
- Provencal herbs (thyme, rosemary, basil) (1 tsp) (1g)
- Garlic, minced (2 cloves) (6g)
- Salt and pepper to taste

Instructions:

1. In a large pot, heat olive oil. Brown beef on all sides. Remove and set aside.

2. Add onions and garlic to the pot, cook until translucent.

3. Return beef to the pot, add vegetables, tomatoes, broth, Provencal herbs, salt, and pepper.

4. Bring to a boil, then reduce heat to low and simmer for 2 hours until beef is tender.

Nutritional Facts (Per Serving): Calories: 450 | Sugars: 6g | Fat: 20g | Carbohydrates: 25g | Protein: 40g | Fiber: 5g | Sodium: 10g

Chicken Rollatini with Feta, Spinach, and Roasted Peppers

Prep: 25 minutes | Cook: 30 minutes | Serves: 4

Ingredients:

- Chicken breasts, pounded thin (4) (600g)
- Feta cheese, crumbled (1/2 cup) (75g)
- Fresh spinach, chopped (1 cup) (30g)
- Olive oil (2 tbsp) (30ml)
- Garlic, minced (2 cloves) (6g)
- Salt and pepper to taste
- Roasted red peppers, sliced (1/2 cup) (100g)

Instructions:

1. Preheat oven to 375°F (190°C).
2. Mix feta, spinach, roasted peppers, and garlic.
3. Place mixture on each chicken breast, roll up, and secure with toothpicks.
4. Season with salt and pepper, then brown in olive oil over medium heat.
5. Transfer to the oven and bake for 25 minutes.

Nutritional Facts (Per Serving): Calories: 450 | Sugars: 2g | Fat: 20g | Carbohydrates: 5g | Protein: 60g | Fiber: 1g | Sodium: 8g

Grilled Chicken with Capers, Lemon Sauce, and a Side of Asparagus

Prep: 15 minutes | Cook: 20 minutes | Serves: 4

Ingredients:

- Chicken breasts (4) (600g)
- Asparagus, trimmed (2 cups) (240g)
- Capers (2 tbsp) (16g)
- Lemon, juiced and zested
- Olive oil (2 tbsp) (30ml)
- Chicken broth (1/2 cup) (120ml)
- Salt and pepper to taste

Instructions:

1. Season chicken with salt and pepper, grill over medium heat until cooked, about 6-7 min. per side.
2. Blanch asparagus in boiling water, then shock in ice water.
3. For the sauce, heat lemon juice, zest, capers, and broth in a pan. Reduce by half.
4. Drizzle olive oil over asparagus, season with salt and pepper, and grill until tender.
5. Serve chicken with lemon caper sauce and grilled asparagus on the side.

Nutritional Facts (Per Serving): Calories: 450 | Sugars: 3g | Fat: 15g | Carbohydrates: 10g | Protein: 65g | Fiber: 2g | Sodium: 7g

Lamb Patties with Mint Sauce and a Greek Salad

Prep: 20 minutes | Cook: 10 minutes | Serves: 4

Ingredients:

- Ground lamb (1 lb) (450g)
- Fresh mint, chopped (1/4 cup) (6g)
- Cucumber, diced (1/2 cup) (100g)
- Cherry tomatoes, halved (1 cup) (150g)
- Red onion, thinly sliced (1/2 cup) (75g)
- Feta cheese, crumbled (1/2 cup) (75g)
- Olive oil (for salad) (2 tbsp) (30ml), (for patties) (1 tbsp) (15ml)
- Lemon juice (2 tbsp) (30ml)
- Salt and pepper to taste

Instructions:

1. Mix ground lamb with half the mint, salt, and pepper. Form into patties.
2. Grill patties over medium heat until cooked to desired doneness, about 5 minutes per side.
3. Combine cucumber, tomatoes, onion, feta, remaining mint, olive oil, lemon juice, salt, and pepper for the salad.
4. Serve lamb patties with mint sauce and Greek salad on the side.

Nutritional Facts (Per Serving): Calories: 500 | Sugars: 4g | Fat: 35g | Carbohydrates: 10g | Protein: 40g | Fiber: 2g | Sodium: 10g

Beef Goulash with Paprika, Tomatoes, and Green Beans

Prep: 15 minutes | Cook: 1 hour 30 minutes | Serves: 4

Ingredients:

- Beef chuck, cubed (1 lb) (450g)
- Green beans, trimmed (2 cups) (200g)
- Onion, chopped (1 cup) (160g)
- Garlic, minced (2 cloves) (6g)
- Canned diced tomatoes (2 cups) (480ml)
- Beef broth (2 cups) (480ml)
- Paprika (2 tbsp) (16g)
- Olive oil (1 tbsp) (15ml)
- Salt and pepper to taste

Instructions:

1. In a large pot, heat olive oil. Brown beef on all sides. Remove and set aside.
2. Add onion and garlic to the pot, cook until softened.
3. Return beef to the pot, add paprika, tomatoes, beef broth, salt, and pepper.
4. Bring to a boil, then reduce heat and simmer for 1 hour.
5. Add green beans and cook for an additional 30 minutes until tender. Adjust seasoning and serve.

Nutritional Facts (Per Serving): Calories: 450 | Sugars: 6g | Fat: 20g | Carbohydrates: 15g | Protein: 50g | Fiber: 4g | Sodium: 10g

Baked Chicken Thighs with Mediterranean Vegetables

Prep: 20 minutes | Cook: 45 minutes | Serves: 4

Ingredients:

- Chicken thighs, bone-in, skin-on (4) (800g)
- Kalamata olives (1/2 cup) (50g)
- Cherry tomatoes (1 cup) (150g)
- Zucchini, sliced (1 cup) (120g)
- Olive oil (2 tbsp) (30ml)
- Garlic, minced (2 cloves) (6g)
- Herbs de Provence (1 tsp) (2g)
- Salt and pepper to taste
- Red bell pepper, sliced (1 cup) (150g)

Instructions:

1. Toss chicken, olives, tomatoes, zucchini, bell pepper, garlic, herbs de Provence, olive oil, salt, and pepper together.
2. Arrange in a single layer in a baking dish.
3. Bake for 45 min, until chicken is cooked through.

Nutritional Facts (Per Serving): Calories: 500 | Sugars: 5g | Fat: 30g | Carbohydrates: 10g | Protein: 45g | Fiber: 3g | Sodium: 10g

Chicken with Artichokes, Wine Sauce, and Sauteed Spinach

Prep: 15 minutes | Cook: 30 minutes | Serves: 4

Ingredients:

- Chicken breasts, skinless and boneless (4) (600g)
- Canned artichoke hearts, drained (1 cup) (240g)
- Dry white wine (1/2 cup) (120ml)
- Salt and pepper to taste
- Garlic, minced (2 cloves)
- Olive oil (2 tbsp) (30ml)
- Chicken broth (1 cup) (240ml)
- Lemon juice (2 tbsp) (30ml)
- Fresh spinach (4 cups) (120g)

Instructions:

1. Season chicken with salt and pepper.
2. In a skillet, heat 1 tbsp olive oil over medium heat. Add chicken and cook until golden on both sides. Remove and set aside.
3. In the same skillet, add garlic, artichokes, and cook for 2 minutes.
4. Deg laze the pan with white wine, then add chicken broth and lemon juice. Bring to a simmer.
5. Return chicken to the skillet, cover, and cook for 20 minutes.
6. In another skillet, heat remaining olive oil. Add spinach and sauté until wilted.
7. Serve chicken topped with artichokes and wine sauce, alongside sautéed spinach.

Nutritional Facts (Per Serving): Calories: 450 | Sugars: 2g | Fat: 15g | Carbohydrates: 10g | Protein: 60g | Fiber: 4g | Sodium: 10g

Lamb Ribs with Grilled Zucchini

Prep Time: 20 minutes (plus marinating) | Cook: 40 minutes | Serves: 4

Ingredients:

- Lamb ribs (1 lb) (450g)
- Zucchini, sliced lengthwise (2 large) (400g)
- Garlic, minced (2 cloves) (6g)
- Fresh thyme (2 tbsp) (6g)
- Olive oil (for ribs) (2 tbsp) (30ml), (for zucchini) (1 tbsp) (15ml)
- Salt and pepper to taste

Instructions:

1. Marinate lamb ribs with garlic, thyme, olive oil, salt, and pepper for at least 2 hours.
2. Preheat grill to medium-high heat.
3. Grill lamb ribs, turning occasionally, until cooked to desired doneness, about 30 minutes.
4. Toss zucchini slices in olive oil, salt, and pepper.
5. Grill until tender, about 10 minutes.
6. Serve lamb ribs with grilled zucchini on the side.

Nutritional Facts (Per Serving): Calories: 500 | Sugars: 4g | Fat: 35g | Carbohydrates: 10g | Protein: 40g | Fiber: 3g | Sodium: 10g

Beef Vegetable Ragout with Herbs and a Quinoa Salad

Prep: 20 minutes | Cook: 1 hour | Serves:4

Ingredients:

- Beef chuck, cubed (1 lb) (450g)
- Carrots, diced (1 cup) (130g)
- Zucchini, diced (1 cup) (120g)
- Onion, chopped (1 cup) (160g)
- Garlic, minced (2 cloves) (6g)
- Salt and pepper to taste
- Canned diced tomatoes (2 cups) (480ml)
- Beef broth (2 cups) (480ml)
- Fresh thyme and rosemary (1 tsp each) (2g each)
- Olive oil (1 tbsp) (15ml)
- Quinoa (1 cup) (170g)
- Lemon juice (2 tbsp) (30ml)
- Fresh parsley, chopped (1/4 cup) (15g)

Instructions:

1. In a large pot, heat olive oil. Add beef and brown on all sides. Remove and set aside.
2. Add onion and garlic to the pot, cook until translucent.
3. Return beef to the pot, add carrots, zucchini, tomatoes, beef broth, thyme, rosemary, salt, and pepper.
4. Bring to a boil, then simmer for 1 hour until beef is tender.
5. Cook quinoa as per package instructions. Toss with lemon juice, parsley, salt, and pepper.
6. Serve ragout over quinoa salad.

Nutritional Facts (Per Serving): Calories: 500 | Sugars: 6g | Fat: 20g | Carbohydrates: 40g | Protein: 40g | Fiber: 6g | Sodium: 10g

Grilled Chicken Fillet with a Tomato-Cucumber Salad

Prep: 15 minutes | Cook: 20 minutes | Serves: 4

Ingredients:

- Chicken breast fillets (4) (600g)
- Fresh rosemary, chopped (2 tbsp) (6g)
- Lemon, juiced and zested
- Cucumber, diced (1 cup) (120g)
- Cherry tomatoes, halved (1 cup) (150g)
- Olive oil (2 tbsp) (30ml)
- Salt and pepper to taste

Instructions:

1. Marinate chicken with lemon juice, zest, rosemary, salt, and pepper for at least 30 minutes.
2. Grill chicken over medium heat until cooked through, about 10 minutes per side.
3. In a bowl, combine cucumber, tomatoes, a drizzle of olive oil, salt, and pepper to make the salad.
4. Serve grilled chicken with tomato-cucumber salad on the side.

Nutritional Facts (Per Serving): Calories: 450 | Sugars: 4g | Fat: 15g | Carbohydrates: 10g | Protein: 65g | Fiber: 2g | Sodium: 10g

Pork in Honey-Mustard Marinade with a Side of Grilled Eggplant

Prep: 20 minutes (plus marinating time) | Cook: 20 minutes | Serves: 4

Ingredients:

- Pork tenderloin (1 lb) (450g)
- Honey (2 tbsp) (40ml)
- Dijon mustard (2 tbsp) (30ml)
- Garlic, minced (2 cloves)
- Salt and pepper to taste
- Olive oil (for marinade) (1 tbsp) (15ml), (for vegetables) (1 tbsp) (15ml)
- Eggplant, sliced (1 medium) (200g)
- Bell peppers, sliced (2) (300g)

Instructions:

1. Whisk together honey, Dijon mustard, garlic, 1 tbsp olive oil, salt, and pepper to create the marinade.
2. Marinate pork tenderloin in the mixture for at least 2 hours in the refrigerator.
3. Preheat grill to medium-high heat.
4. Grill pork tenderloin, turning occasionally, until cooked through, about 15-20 minutes.
5. Toss eggplant and bell peppers with 1 tbsp olive oil, salt, and pepper.
6. Grill vegetables until tender and charred, about 10 minutes. Let pork rest for 5 minutes, then slice.
8. Serve sliced pork with grilled eggplant and bell peppers on the side.

Nutritional Facts (Per Serving): Calories: 450 | Sugars: 10g | Fat: 15g | Carbohydrates: 20g | Protein: 50g | Fiber: 5g | Sodium: 10g

Zucchini Baked with Parmesan

Prep: 10 minutes | Cook: 20 minutes | Serves: 4

Ingredients:

- Zucchini, sliced (2 medium) (800g)
- Parmesan cheese, grated (1/2 cup) (25g)
- Olive oil (1 tbsp) (15ml)
- Fresh herbs (thyme, oregano) (1 tsp) (2g)
- Salt and pepper to taste

Instructions:

1. Preheat oven to 375°F (190°C).
2. Arrange zucchini slices in a single layer on a baking sheet.
3. Drizzle with olive oil, sprinkle with salt, pepper, herbs, and Parmesan cheese.
4. Bake for 20 minutes, until tender and cheese is golden brown. Serve hot.

Nutritional Facts (Per Serving): Calories: 220 | Sugars: 4g | Fat: 15g | Carbohydrates: 30g | Protein: 20g | Fiber: 3g | Sodium: 10g

Olive Tapenade with Whole Grain Bread

Prep: 10 minutes | Cook: 0 minutes | Serves: 4

Ingredients:

- Black olives, pitted (1 cup) (150g)
- Capers, rinsed (1 tbsp) (8g)
- Olive oil (2 tbsp) (30ml)
- Garlic, minced (1 clove) (3g)
- Lemon juice (1 tbsp) (15ml)
- Fresh parsley, chopped (1 tbsp) (4g)
- Whole grain bread, sliced (4 slices) (160g)

Instructions:

1. In a food processor, blend olives, capers, olive oil, garlic, lemon juice, and parsley until smooth.
2. Serve tapenade spread over whole grain bread slices.

Nutritional Facts (Per Serving): Calories: 200 | Sugars: 1g | Fat: 15g | Carbohydrates: 15g | Protein: 3g | Fiber: 3g | Sodium: 300mg

Eggplant Caviar with Garlic and Herbs

Feta Cheese Marinated with Olive Oil and Herbs

Prep: 15 minutes | Cook: 40 minutes | Serves: 4

Prep: 10 minutes (plus marinating time) | Cook: 0 minutes | Serves: 4

Ingredients:

- Eggplant (1 large) (450g)
- Olive oil (2 tbsp) (30ml)
- Garlic, minced (3 cloves) (9g)
- Fresh parsley, chopped (1/4 cup) (15g)
- Fresh lemon juice (1 tbsp) (15ml)
- Salt and pepper to taste

Ingredients:

- Feta cheese (8 oz) (225g)
- Olive oil (3 tbsp) (45ml)
- Fresh thyme (1 tbsp) (3g)
- Fresh rosemary (1 tbsp) (3g)
- Red pepper flakes (1/2 tsp) (1g)
- Lemon zest (from 1 lemon)
- Garlic, minced (2 cloves) (6g)

Instructions:

1. Preheat oven to 400°F (200°C). Pierce eggplants with a fork and bake until tender, about 40 minutes.
2. Scoop out the eggplant flesh and chop finely.
3. Mix eggplant with olive oil, garlic, parsley, lemon juice, salt, and pepper.
4. Serve chilled or at room temperature.

Instructions:

1. Cut feta into cubes and place in a shallow dish.
2. Combine olive oil, thyme, rosemary, garlic, red pepper flakes, and lemon zest. Pour over feta.
3. Marinate for at least 4 hours or overnight in the refrigerator.
4. Serve with whole grain bread or crackers.

Nutritional Facts (Per Serving): Calories: 220 | Sugars: 5g | Fat: 14g | Carbohydrates: 22g | Protein: 3g | Fiber: 6g | Sodium: 10mg

Nutritional Facts (Per Serving): 200 | Sugars: 0g | Fat: 18g | Carbohydrates: 2g | Protein: 6g | Fiber: 0g | Sodium: 400mg

Bruschetta with Tomatoes, Basil, and Mozzarella

Prep: 15 minutes | Cook: 5 minutes | Serves: 4

Ingredients:

- Roma tomatoes, diced (2 medium) (200g)
- Fresh mozzarella, diced (1/2 cup) (60g)
- Fresh basil, chopped (1/4 cup) (15g)
- Olive oil (2 tbsp) (30ml)
- Balsamic vinegar (1 tbsp) (15ml)
- Garlic, minced (1 clove) (3g)
- Salt and pepper to taste

Instructions:

1. Toast baguette slices until lightly golden.
2. In a bowl, mix tomatoes, mozzarella, basil, olive oil, balsamic vinegar, garlic, salt, and pepper.
3. Spoon tomato mixture onto toasted baguette slices.
4. Serve immediately.

Nutritional Facts (Per Serving): Calories: 220 | Sugars: 3g | Fat: 10g | Carbohydrates: 22g | Protein: 8g | Fiber: 2g | Sodium: 300mg

Tartlets with Caramelized Onion and Brie Cheese

Prep: 15 minutes | Cook: 25 minutes | Serves: 4

Ingredients:

- Pre-made tartlet shells (8) (160g)
- Brie cheese, sliced (1/2 cup) (60g)
- Onion, thinly sliced (1 large) (150g)
- Olive oil (1 tbsp) (15ml)
- Balsamic vinegar (1 tsp) (5ml)
- Thyme, fresh (1 tsp) (1g)
- Salt and pepper to taste

Instructions:

1. Preheat oven to 375°F (190°C).
2. In a pan, heat olive oil over medium heat. Add onions, salt, and pepper. Cook until caramelized, about 15 minutes. Stir in balsamic vinegar and thyme.
3. Place tartlet shells on a baking sheet. Fill each shell with caramelized onions and top with a slice of Brie cheese.
4. Bake for 10 minutes, until cheese is melted and bubbly.
5. Serve warm.

Nutritional Facts (Per Serving): Calories: 210 | Sugars: 5g | Fat: 14g | Carbohydrates: 18g | Protein: 5g | Fiber: 1g | Sodium: 200mg

Falafel with Tahini Sauce

Prep:20 minutes (plus soaking time) | Cook: 10 minutes | Serves: 4

Ingredients:

- Dried chickpeas, soaked overnight (1 cup) (164g)
- Onion, chopped (1 medium) (160g)
- Garlic, minced (2 cloves) (6g)
- Fresh parsley, chopped (1/4 cup) (15g)
- Salt and pepper to taste
- Olive oil for frying
- Tahini (1/4 cup) (60ml)
- Lemon juice (1 tbsp) (15ml)
- Water (as needed)
- Cumin (1 tsp) (2g)

Instructions:

1. Drain chickpeas and blend with onion, garlic, parsley, cumin, salt, and pepper until smooth. Form into small balls.
2. Heat olive oil in a pan and fry falafel balls until golden on all sides.
3. For the tahini sauce, mix tahini and lemon juice, adding water as needed for desired consistency.
4. Serve falafel with tahini sauce on the side.

Nutritional Facts (Per Serving): Calories: 220 | Sugars: 3g | Fat: 14g | Carbohydrates: 18g | Protein: 6g | Fiber: 5g | Sodium: 200mg

Whole Grain Crackers with Avocado and Tomato Salsa

Prep: 10 minutes | Cook: 0 minutes | Serves: 4

Ingredients:

- Whole grain crackers (4 crackers) (60g)
- Avocado, diced (1/2 avocado) (100g)
- Cherry tomatoes, diced (1 cup) (100g)
- Lime juice (2 tbsp) (30ml)
- Cilantro, chopped (1/4 cup) (4g)
- Salt and pepper to taste
- Red onion, finely chopped (1/4 cup) (40g)

Instructions:

1. In a bowl, combine mashed avocados, diced cherry tomatoes, chopped red onion, lime juice, cilantro, salt, and pepper.
2. Mix well to combine.
3. Serve the avocado and tomato salsa with whole grain crackers on the side.

Nutritional Facts (Per Serving): Calories: 200 | Sugars: 2g | Fat: 12g | Carbohydrates: 20g | Protein: 3g | Fiber: 5g | Sodium: 100mg

Eggplant Rolls with Cheese and Tomatoes

Prep Time: 20 minutes | Cook: 15 minutes | Serves: 4

Ingredients:

- Eggplants, thinly sliced lengthwise (1 large) (250g)
- Ricotta cheese (1/2 cup) (120g)
- Parmesan cheese, grated (1/4 cup) (25g)
- Cherry tomatoes, halved (1/2 cup) (100g)
- Fresh basil, chopped (1/4 cup) (15g)
- Olive oil (2 tbsp) (30ml)
- Salt and pepper to taste

Instructions:

1. Preheat oven to 375°F (190°C).
2. Brush eggplant slices with olive oil, season with salt and pepper, and grill until tender.
3. Mix ricotta, Parmesan, basil, and a pinch of salt and pepper.
4. Place a tablespoon of cheese mixture on one end of each eggplant slice, add a couple of tomato halves, and roll up.
5. Arrange eggplant rolls in a baking dish and bake for 15 minutes.
6. Serve warm.

Nutritional Facts (Per Serving): Calories: 210 | Sugars: 5g | Fat: 14g | Carbohydrates: 15g | Protein: 8g | Fiber: 4g | Sodium: 200mg

Baked Sweet Potato Chips with Greek Yogurt

Prep: 10 minutes | Cook: 20 minutes | Serves: 4

Ingredients:

- Sweet potato, thinly sliced (2 medium) (300g)
- Olive oil (1 tbsp) (15ml)
- Greek yogurt (for serving) (1/2 cup) (120g)
- Salt and pepper to taste

Instructions:

1. Preheat oven to 400°F (200°C). Line a baking sheet with parchment paper.
2. Toss sweet potato slices with olive oil, salt, and pepper. Arrange in a single layer on the baking sheet.
3. Bake for 20 minutes, turning halfway through, until crispy.
4. Serve with a side of Greek yogurt for dipping.

Nutritional Facts (Per Serving): Calories: 220 | Sugars: 5g | Fat: 5g | Carbohydrates: 35g | Protein: 6g | Fiber: 5g | Sodium: 150mg

CHAPTER 12: DESSERTS: Fresh and Fruity

Fresh Figs with Goat Cheese and Honey

Prep: 5 minutes | Cook: 0 minutes | Serves: 4

Ingredients:

- Fresh figs, halved (8) (400g)
- Goat cheese (1/2 cup) (120g)
- Honey (2 tbsp) (30ml)
- Fresh thyme (1 tsp) (1g)

Instructions:

1. Place halved figs on a serving plate.
2. Spoon a dollop of goat cheese onto each fig half.
3. Drizzle honey over the figs and goat cheese.
4. Garnish with fresh thyme.

Nutritional Facts (Per Serving): Calories: 200 | Sugars: 18g | Fat: 8g | Carbohydrates: 28g | Protein: 6g | Fiber: 3g | Sodium: 45mg

Fresh Berry Sorbet

Prep: 10 minutes (plus freezing time) | Cook: 0 minutes | Serves: 4

Ingredients:

- Mixed fresh berries (strawberries, raspberries, blueberries) (2 cups) (300g)
- Lemon juice (1 tbsp) (15 ml)
- Water (1/4 cup) (60ml)
- Honey (2 tbsp) (30ml)

Instructions:

1. Blend berries, honey, lemon juice, and water until smooth.
2. Strain mixture to remove seeds, if desired.
3. Pour into a shallow dish and freeze until firm, stirring every 30 minutes.
4. Serve sorbet scoops in bowls.

Nutritional Facts (Per Serving): Calories: 210 | Sugars: 24g | Fat: 1g | Carbohydrates: 50g | Protein: 2g | Fiber: 4g | Sodium: 5mg

Apple Charlotte with Cinnamon

Prep: 20 minutes | Cook: 35 minutes | Serves: 4

Ingredients:

- Apples, peeled and sliced (3 medium) (300g)
- Brown sugar (2 tbsp) (30g)
- Cinnamon (1 tsp) (2g)
- Bread slices, crusts removed (6) (180g)
- Butter, melted (2 tbsp) (30ml)

Instructions:

1. Preheat oven to 375°F (190°C).
2. Toss apples with brown sugar and cinnamon.
3. Line a baking dish with buttered bread slices, overlapping slightly.
4. Fill with the apple mixture and top with more bread slices, buttered side up.
5. Bake until golden and bubbly, about 35 minutes.
6. Serve warm.

Nutritional Facts (Per Serving): Calories: 220 | Sugars: 22g | Fat: 7g | Carbohydrates: 35g | Protein: 4g | Fiber: 5g | Sodium: 150mg

Ricotta Cream with Berries and Honey

Prep: 10 minutes | Cook: 0 minutes | Serves: 4

Ingredients:

- Ricotta cheese (1 cups) (250g)
- Mixed berries (strawberries, blueberries, raspberries) (1 cups) (150g)
- Vanilla extract (1 tsp) (5ml)
- Lemon zest (1 tsp) (2g)
- Honey (2 tbsp) (30ml)

Instructions:

1. In a mixing bowl, combine ricotta cheese, vanilla extract, and lemon zest. Stir until smooth.
2. Divide the ricotta mixture among four serving dishes.
3. Top each with a generous portion of mixed berries.
4. Drizzle honey over the berries and ricotta cream.
5. Serve immediately or chill in the refrigerator until ready to serve.

Nutritional Facts (Per Serving): Calories: 200 | Sugars: 15g | Fat: 8g | Carbohydrates: 20g | Protein: 10g | Fiber: 2g | Sodium: 80mg

Low-Sugar Tiramisu with Whole Grain Biscuits

Prep: 20 minutes | Cook: 0 minutes | Chill: 2 hours | Serves: 4

Ingredients:

- Whole grain biscuits (12 biscuits) (120g)
- Mascarpone cheese (1/2 cup) (120g)
- Heavy cream (1/4 cup) (60ml)
- Strong brewed coffee, cooled (1/2 cup) (120ml)
- Cocoa powder for dusting (2 tbsp) (15g)
- Vanilla extract (1 tsp) (5ml)
- Low-sugar sweetener (2 tbsp) (30g)

Instructions:

1. Whip heavy cream, vanilla extract, and sweetener until stiff peaks form.
2. Gently fold in mascarpone cheese until well combined.
3. Briefly dip whole grain biscuits into the coffee and lay them in a single layer in a dish.
4. Spread half of the mascarpone mixture over the biscuits.
5. Add another layer of coffee-dipped biscuits and cover with the remaining mascarpone mixture.
6. Chill in the refrigerator for at least 2 hours.
7. Before serving, dust with cocoa powder.

Nutritional Facts (Per Serving): Calories: 220 | Sugars: 3g | Fat: 16g | Carbohydrates: 15g | Protein: 5g | Fiber: 2g | Sodium: 100mg

Almond Cookies with Citrus Zest

Prep: 15 minutes | Cook: 10 minutes | Serves: 4

Ingredients:

- Ground almonds (1 cup) (100g)
- Low-sugar sweetener (1/4 cup) (50g)
- Egg white (1) (30g)
- Orange zest (1 tbsp) (6g)
- Lemon zest (1 tbsp) (6g)

Instructions:

1. Preheat oven to 350°F (175°C).
2. Mix ground almonds, sweetener, egg white, orange zest, and lemon zest until a dough forms.
3. Form the dough into small balls and place on a baking sheet lined with parchment paper.
4. Bake for 10 minutes or until lightly golden.
5. Let cool before serving.

Nutritional Facts (Per Serving): Calories: 200 | Sugars: 2g | Fat: 15g | Carbohydrates: 8g | Protein: 6g | Fiber: 3g | Sodium: 20mg

Nut Halva with Honey and Sesame

Prep: 15 minutes | Cook: 10 minutes | Serves: 4

Ingredients:

- Mixed nuts (walnuts, almonds) (1 cup) (120g)
- Honey (2 tbsp) (30ml)
- Sesame seeds (1/4 cup) (30g)
- Water (1/4 cup) (60ml)

Instructions:

1. Coarsely grind the mixed nuts.
2. In a pan, toast sesame seeds until golden, then set aside.
3. In the same pan, heat honey and water until slightly thickened.
4. Add the ground nuts and toasted sesame seeds to the honey mixture, stirring until well combined.
5. Pour the mixture into a greased dish or mold. Allow to set until firm, then cut into pieces.
6. Serve at room temperature.

Nutritional Facts (Per Serving): Calories: 220 | Sugars: 10g | Fat: 16g | Carbohydrates: 18g | Protein: 6g | Fiber: 3g | Sodium: 10mg

Avocado-Based Chocolate Mousse

Prep: 10 minutes | Chill: 1 hour | Serves: 4

Ingredients:

- Ripe avocados (1 large) (200g)
- Cocoa powder (1/4 cup) (20g)
- Honey or maple syrup (3 tbsp) (45ml)
- Vanilla extract (1 tsp) (5ml)
- Sea salt (a pinch)

Instructions:

1. Blend avocados, cocoa powder, honey/maple syrup, vanilla extract, and a pinch of sea salt in a food processor until smooth.
2. Divide the mousse among serving dishes.
3. Chill in the refrigerator for at least 1 hour.
4. Serve cold.

Nutritional Facts (Per Serving): Calories: 210 | Sugars: 12g | Fat: 15g | Carbohydrates: 20g | Protein: 3g | Fiber: 7g | Sodium: 20mg

Lemon Curd with Berries

Prep: 10 minutes | Cook: 10 minutes | Serves: 4

Ingredients:

- Lemons, juiced and zested (2 lemons) (100ml juice, 10g zest)
- Sugar (1/4 cup) (50g)
- Egg yolks (2 large) (40g)
- Unsalted butter, cubed (2 tbsp) (30g)
- Mixed berries (strawberries, blueberries, raspberries) (1 cup) (150g)

Instructions:

1. Whisk together lemon juice, sugar, and eggs in a saucepan over low heat.
2. Add butter and stir continuously until the mixture thickens, about 10 minutes.
3. Remove from heat, strain through a fine sieve, and let cool.
4. Serve the lemon curd with fresh berries on top.

Nutritional Facts (Per Serving): Calories: 220 | Sugars: 18g | Fat: 12g | Carbohydrates: 25g | Protein: 2g | Fiber: 2g | Sodium: 20mg

Baklava with Nuts and Honey in Moderation

Prep: 30 minutes | Cook: 50 minutes | Serves: 4

Ingredients:

- Phyllo dough sheets (8) (150g)
- Mixed nuts (walnuts, pistachios, almonds), chopped (1/2 cup) (60g)
- Butter, melted (3 tbsp) (45ml)
- Cinnamon (1 tsp) (2g)
- Water (1/4 cup) (60ml)
- Honey (1/4 cup) (60ml)

Instructions:

1. Preheat oven to 350°F (175°C).
2. Layer 4 phyllo sheets, brushing each with melted butter. Sprinkle half of the nuts and cinnamon.
3. Repeat with the remaining phyllo sheets and nuts.
4. Cut into squares or diamonds before baking.
5. Bake for 50 minutes until golden and crisp.
6. Heat honey and water in a saucepan. Pour over the hot baklava.
7. Let cool before serving.

Nutritional Facts (Per Serving): Calories: 220 | Sugars: 15g | Fat: 15g | Carbohydrates: 20g | Protein: 4g | Fiber: 2g | Sodium: 150mg

CHAPTER 14: DESSERTS: Traditional Mediterranean Desserts Reimagined

Panna Cotta with Lavender Syrup

Prep: 15 minutes | Cook: 5 minutes | Chill: 4 hours | Serves: 4

Ingredients:

- Heavy cream (1 cups) (240ml)
- Sugar (1/4 cup) (50g)
- Gelatin powder (1 tsp) (3g)
- Vanilla extract (1 tsp) (5ml)
- **For the lavender syrup**: Dried lavender flowers (1 tbsp) (1g)
- Honey (2 tbsp) (30ml)
- Water (1/4 cup) (60ml)

Instructions:

1. Sprinkle gelatin over water in a bowl to soften.
2. Heat heavy cream and sugar in a saucepan until sugar dissolves. Remove from heat.
3. Stir in softened gelatin and vanilla until gelatin dissolves.
4. Pour into serving glasses and chill until set, about 4 hours.
5. For the syrup, combine lavender, sugar, and water in a saucepan. Simmer until sugar dissolves.
6. Strain and cool.
7. Serve panna cotta with lavender syrup drizzled on top.

Nutritional Facts (Per Serving): Calories: 210 | Sugars: 18g | Fat: 15g | Carbohydrates: 16g | Protein: 2g | Fiber: 0g | Sodium: 20mg

Olive Oil Cake with Lemon Glaze

Prep: 20 minutes | Cook: 45 minutes | Serves: 8

Ingredients:

- All-purpose flour (1 1/2 cups) (180g)
- Sugar (3/4 cup) (150g)
- Olive oil (1/2 cup) (120ml)
- Eggs (2 large)
- Lemon zest (from 1 lemon)
- Baking powder (1 tsp) (4g)
- Salt (1/2 tsp) (2g)

For the glaze:
- Powdered sugar (1 cup) (120g)
- Lemon juice (2 tbsp) (30ml)

Instructions:

1. Preheat oven to 350°F (175°C). Grease and flour a cake pan.
2. Mix flour, baking powder, and salt. In another bowl, whisk sugar, olive oil, eggs, and lemon zest.
3. Combine wet and dry ingredients until smooth.

4. Pour into the prepared pan and bake for 45 minutes.

5. For the glaze, mix powdered sugar and lemon juice until smooth. Drizzle over the cooled cake.

Nutritional Facts (Per Serving): Calories: 220 | Sugars: 20g | Fat: 12g | Carbohydrates: 25g | Protein: 3g | Fiber: 1g | Sodium: 150mg

Orange Phyllo Tartlets with Honey

Prep: 20 minutes | Cook: 15 minutes | Serves: 4

Ingredients:

- Phyllo dough sheets (4) (60g)
- Butter, melted (2 tbsp) (30ml)
- Fresh oranges, segmented (2 medium) (300g)
- Honey (2 tbsp) (30ml)
- Ground cinnamon (1 tsp) (2g)

Instructions:

1. Preheat oven to 375°F (190°C). Cut phyllo sheets into squares and layer into muffin tins, brushing each layer with melted butter.

2. Bake phyllo cups until golden, about 10-15 min.

3. Allow to cool, then fill each cup with orange segments.

4. Drizzle with honey and sprinkle with cinnamon before serving.

Nutritional Facts (Per Serving): Calories: 210 | Sugars: 15g | Fat: 10g | Carbohydrates: 25g | Protein: 3g | Fiber: 2g | Sodium: 10mg

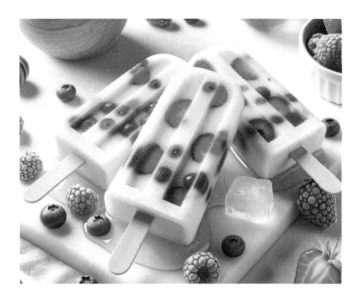

Yogurt Popsicles with Berries and Honey

Prep: 15 minutes | Freeze: 4 hours | Serves: 6

Ingredients:

- Greek yogurt (1 cup) (240g)
- Mixed berries (strawberries, blueberries, raspberries) (1/2 cup) (75g)
- Honey (3 tbsp) (60ml)
- Vanilla extract (1 tsp) (5ml)

Instructions:

1. In a bowl, mix Greek yogurt, honey, and vanilla extract until well combined.

2. Gently fold in the mixed berries, keeping some berries whole.

3. Spoon the mixture into popsicle molds, inserting sticks when partially filled if necessary.

4. Freeze for at least 4 hours or until solid.

5. To release popsicles, run warm water over the outside of the molds for a few seconds.

6. Serve immediately for a refreshing treat.

Nutritional Facts (Per Serving): Calories: 200 | Sugars: 18g | Fat: 3g | Carbohydrates: 35g | Protein: 8g | Fiber: 2g | Sodium: 50mg

Pie with Figs and Almonds

Prep: 15 minutes | Cook: 30 minutes | Serves: 4

Ingredients:

- Whole wheat flour (1 cup) (120g)
- Almond flour (1/2 cup) (48g)
- Unsalted butter, chilled and cubed (1/4 cup) (60g)
- Water (2-3 tbsp) (30-45ml)
- Fresh figs, sliced (6 figs) (300g)
- Honey (2 tbsp) (30ml)
- Sliced almonds (1/4 cup) (23g)
- Cinnamon (1 tsp) (2g)

Instructions:

1. Preheat oven to 375°F (190°C).
2. In a bowl, mix whole wheat flour and almond flour.
3. Add butter and mix until crumbly. Gradually add water to form dough.
4. Press dough into a pie pan. Chill for 10 minutes. Arrange fig slices over the crust.
5. Drizzle with honey and sprinkle with cinnamon and almonds.
6. Bake for 30 minutes or until crust is golden.

Nutritional Facts (Per Serving): Calories: 210 | Sugars: 15g | Fat: 10g | Carbohydrates: 27g | Protein: 5g | Fiber: 4g | Sodium: 5mg

Mango and Coconut Milk Mousse

Prep: 15 minutes | Chill: 2 hours | Serves: 4

Ingredients:

- Ripe mango, pureed (1 large) (200g)
- Light coconut milk (1 cup) (240ml)
- Honey (1 tbsp) (15ml)
- Gelatin powder (1 tsp) (3g)
- Lime juice (1 tbsp) (15ml)

Instructions:

1. Sprinkle gelatin over lime juice and let sit for 5 minutes to bloom.
2. Gently heat a portion of coconut milk and dissolve the bloomed gelatin in it.
3. Blend mango puree with the remaining coconut milk and honey.
4. Mix in the gelatin-coconut milk mixture.
5. Pour into molds or cups and refrigerate for at least 2 hours to set.
6. Serve chilled, garnished with mango slices or lime zest.

Nutritional Facts (Per Serving): Calories: 200 | Sugars: 18g | Fat: 8g | Carbohydrates: 28g | Protein: 2g | Fiber: 1g | Sodium: 15mg

CHAPTER 15: DINNER: Flavor-Packed Vegetable Sides

Ratatouille in a Skillet with Minimal Olive Oil

Prep: 20 minutes | Cook: 30 minutes | Serves: 4

Ingredients:

- Zucchini (1 large) (200g)
- Eggplant (1 medium) (200g)
- Bell peppers (1 each of red, yellow, green) (450g total)
- Onion (1 medium) (160g)
- Garlic cloves (2) (6g)
- Olive oil (2 tbsp) (30ml)
- Fresh thyme (1 tsp) (1g)
- Salt and pepper to taste
- Tomatoes (2 large) (400g)

Instructions:

1. Chop all vegetables into bite-sized pieces.
2. Heat olive oil in a large skillet over medium heat.
3. Add garlic and onion, cooking until translucent.
4. Add eggplant and bell peppers, cook for 5 minutes.
5. Add zucchini and tomatoes, season with thyme, salt, and pepper. Stir well.
6. Cover and simmer for 20 minutes, stirring occasionally, until vegetables are tender.

Nutritional Facts (Per Serving): Calories: 450 | Sugars: 20g | Fat: 7g | Carbohydrates: 80g | Protein: 10g | Fiber: 20g | Sodium: 10g

Spinach Pie with Low-Fat Feta (Spanakopita)

Prep: 20 minutes | Cook: 30 minutes | Serves: 4

Ingredients:

- Fresh spinach, chopped (4 cups) (400g)
- Low-fat feta cheese, crumbled (1 cup) (150g)
- Phyllo dough sheets (6 sheets) (90g)
- Salt and pepper to taste
- Onion, finely chopped (1 small) (100g)
- Garlic cloves, minced (2 cloves) (6g)
- Olive oil (2 tbsp) (30ml)
- Egg, beaten (1 large)
- Nutmeg (1/4 tsp) (0.5g)

Instructions:

1. Preheat oven to 375°F (190°C).
2. Sauté onion and garlic in 1 tbsp olive oil until soft. Add spinach and cook until wilted.
3. Remove from heat, let cool, then mix in feta, egg, nutmeg, salt, and pepper.

4. Brush a baking dish with olive oil.

5. Lay 2 phyllo sheets, brush with olive oil, repeat layering with remaining sheets.

6. Spread spinach mixture over phyllo. Fold overhanging phyllo over the filling.

7. Brush the top with olive oil.

8. Bake for 30 minutes, until golden brown.

Nutritional Information (Per Serving): Calories: 390 | Sugars: 3g | Fat: 17g | Carbohydrates: 40g | Protein: 20g | Fiber: 4g | Sodium: 500mg

Pasta Primavera with Seasonal Vegetables, Whole Wheat Pasta

Prep: 15 minutes | Cook: 20 minutes | Serves: 4

Ingredients:

- Whole wheat pasta (8 oz) (225g)
- Asparagus, trimmed and cut into pieces (1 cup) (135g)
- Broccoli florets (1 cup) (150g)
- Carrots, julienned (1/2 cup) (65g)
- Bell pepper, sliced (1 medium) (150g)
- Cherry tomatoes, halved (1 cup) (150g)
- Garlic, minced (2 cloves) (6g)
- Olive oil (2 tbsp) (30ml)
- Fresh basil, chopped (1/4 cup) (15g)
- Parmesan cheese, grated (1/4 cup) (25g)
- Salt and pepper to taste

Instructions:

1. Cook whole wheat pasta according to package instructions. Drain and set aside.

2. In a large skillet, heat olive oil over medium heat.

3. Add garlic, asparagus, broccoli, carrots, and bell pepper. Sauté until vegetables are just tender, about 5-7 minutes.

4. Add cherry tomatoes and cook for an additional 2 minutes.

5. Toss cooked vegetables with the pasta, fresh basil, and Parmesan cheese. Season with salt and pepper to taste.

6. Serve warm.

Nutritional Facts (Per Serving): Calories: 450 | Sugars: 6g | Fat: 10g | Carbohydrates: 70g | Protein: 20g | Fiber: 10g | Sodium: 10g

CHAPTER 16: DINNER: Refreshing and Nutritious Salads

Niçoise Salad with Grilled Tuna and a Few Anchovies

Prep: 20 minutes | Cook: 10 minutes | Serves: 4

Ingredients:

- Fresh tuna steaks (4) (600g)
- Mixed salad greens (4 cups) (120g)
- Green beans, trimmed and blanched (1 cup) (150g)
- Small potatoes, boiled and quartered (2 cups) (300g)
- Black olives (1/4 cup) (30g)
- Anchovy fillets (8) (40g)
- For the dressing: Olive oil (1/4 cup) (60ml), Lemon juice (2 tbsp) (30ml), Dijon mustard (1 tsp) (5ml), Salt and pepper to taste
- Cherry tomatoes, halved (1 cup) (150g)

Instructions:

1. Grill tuna steaks over medium heat until cooked to desired doneness, about 4-5 minutes per side.
2. Arrange salad greens on a platter. Top with green beans, potatoes, cherry tomatoes, olives.
3. Slice grilled tuna and arrange on top of the salad.
4. Distribute anchovies evenly.
5. Whisk together olive oil, lemon juice, Dijon mustard, salt, and pepper for the dressing.
6. Serve immediately.

Nutritional Facts (Per Serving): Calories: 450 | Sugars: 4g | Fat: 20g | Carbohydrates: 30g | Protein: 40g | Fiber: 5g | Sodium: 10g, and

Mediterranean Roasted Vegetable Salad with Low-Fat Feta, Pine Nuts

Prep: 15 minutes | Cook: 25 minutes | Serves: 4

Ingredients:

- Zucchini, sliced (2 medium) (400g)
- Bell pepper, sliced (1 large) (150g)
- Red onion, sliced (1 medium) (160g)
- Cherry tomatoes (1 cup) (150g)
- Pine nuts, toasted (1/4 cup) (30g)
- Olive oil (2 tbsp) (30ml)
- Balsamic vinegar (2 tbsp) (30ml)
- Salt and pepper to taste
- Low-fat feta cheese, crumbled (1 cup) (150g)

Instructions:

1. Preheat oven to 425°F (220°C). Toss zucchini, bell pepper, onion, and cherry tomatoes with olive oil, salt, and pepper.
2. Spread vegetables on a baking sheet and roast until tender, about 25 minutes.
3. Let vegetables cool slightly, then transfer to a

serving bowl.

4. Add crumbled feta and pine nuts.

5. Drizzle with balsamic vinegar and serve.

Nutritional Facts (Per Serving): Calories: 450 | Sugars: 10g | Fat: 25g | Carbohydrates: 40g | Protein: 20g | Fiber: 6g | Sodium: 10g

Warm Quinoa Salad with Grilled Eggplant and Sun-Dried Tomatoes

Prep: 15 minutes | Cook: 20 minutes | Serves: 4

Ingredients:

- Quinoa (1 cup) (170g)
- Eggplant, sliced (1 large) (300g)
- Sun-dried tomatoes, chopped (1/2 cup) (55g)
- Olive oil (2 tbsp) (30ml)
- Lemon juice (2 tbsp) (30ml)
- Fresh basil, chopped (1/4 cup) (15g)
- Salt and pepper to taste

Instructions:

1. Cook quinoa according to package instructions.
2. Set aside.
3. Grill eggplant slices brushed with olive oil until tender and slightly charred, about 3-4 min. per side.
4. In a large bowl, combine cooked quinoa, grilled eggplant, sun-dried tomatoes, lemon juice, basil, salt, and pepper. Serve the salad warm.

Nutritional Facts (Per Serving): Calories: 450 | Sugars: 5g | Fat: 15g | Carbohydrates: 65g | Protein: 15g | Fiber: 10g | Sodium: 10g

Avocado and Orange Citrus Salad with Mint Dressing

Prep: 15 minutes | Cook: 0 minutes | Serves: 4

Ingredients:

- Avocados, sliced (2 medium) (400g)
- Oranges, peeled and segmented (3 medium) (450g)
- Mixed salad greens (4 cups) (120g)
- Fresh mint leaves, finely chopped (1/4 cup) (15g)
- Olive oil (3 tbsp) (45ml)
- Honey (1 tbsp) (15ml)
- Lemon juice (2 tbsp) (30ml)
- Salt and pepper to taste
- For the Mint Dressing

Instructions:

1. In a small bowl, whisk together mint leaves, olive oil, honey, lemon juice, salt, and pepper to create the dressing.
2. In a large salad bowl, combine mixed greens, avocado slices, and orange segments.
3. Drizzle the mint dressing over the salad and gently toss to combine.
4. Serve immediately, ensuring even distribution of avocados and oranges in each serving.

Nutritional Facts (Per Serving): Calories: 450 | Sugars: 15g | Fat: 30g | Carbohydrates: 40g | Protein: 5g | Fiber: 10g | Sodium: 5g

CHAPTER 17: DINNER: Evening Meals A Mediterranean Feast

Baked Salmon with Thyme and Lemon

Prep: 10 minutes | Cook: 20 minutes | Serves: 2

Ingredients:

- Salmon fillets (2) (300g each)
- Fresh thyme (1 tbsp) (1g)
- Lemon, thinly sliced (1 medium)
- Olive oil (1 tbsp) (15ml)
- Salt and pepper to taste

Instructions:

1. Preheat the oven to 375°F (190°C).
2. Place salmon on a baking sheet lined with parchment paper. Drizzle with olive oil, and season with salt and pepper.
3. Top each fillet with fresh thyme and lemon slices.
4. Bake for 20 minutes, or until salmon is cooked through and flakes easily.
5. Serve immediately.

Nutritional Facts (Per Serving): Calories: 450 | Sugars: 0g | Fat: 30g | Carbohydrates: 0g | Protein: 45g | Fiber: 0g | Sodium: 5g

Orecchiette with Broccoli, Garlic, and Olive Oil, Whole Wheat Pasta

Prep: 10 minutes | Cook: 20 minutes | Serves: 4

Ingredients:

- Whole wheat orecchiette pasta (8 oz) (225g)
- Broccoli florets (2 cups) (200g)
- Garlic, minced (3 cloves) (9g)
- Red pepper flakes (1/2 tsp) (1g)
- Salt and pepper to taste
- Grated Parmesan cheese (for serving) (1/4 cup) (25g)
- Olive oil (2 tbsp) (30ml)

Instructions:

1. Cook pasta according to package instructions. In the last 3 minutes of cooking, add broccoli florets.
2. Drain pasta and broccoli, reserving some cooking water.
3. In the same pot, heat olive oil over medium heat.
4. Add garlic and red pepper flakes, cooking until fragrant.
5. Add pasta and broccoli back to the pot, tossing with olive oil and garlic. Add a little pasta water to create a light sauce.

6. Season with salt and pepper, and serve with grated Parmesan on top.

Nutritional Facts (Per Serving): Calories: 450 | Sugars: 2g | Fat: 15g | Carbohydrates: 65g | Protein: 20g | Fiber: 10g | Sodium: 10g

Pasta with Basil Pesto and Pine Nuts, Whole Wheat

Prep:15 minutes | Cook: 10 minutes | Serves: 4

Ingredients:

- Whole wheat pasta (8 oz) (225g)
- Basil pesto (1/2 cup) (120ml)
- Pine nuts, toasted (1/4 cup) (30g)
- Fresh basil leaves (for garnish)
- Grated Parmesan cheese (for serving) (1/4 cup) (25g)

Instructions:

1. Cook pasta according to package instructions. Drain and return to pot.
2. Stir in basil pesto until pasta is evenly coated.
3. Serve pasta topped with toasted pine nuts, extra basil leaves, and a sprinkle of Parmesan cheese.

Nutritional Facts (Per Serving): Calories: 450 | Sugars: 3g | Fat: 20g | Carbohydrates: 55g | Protein: 15g | Fiber: 8g | Sodium: 10g

Whole Grain Mini Pizza with Low-Fat Mozzarella and Tomatoes

Prep: 15 minutes | Cook: 10 minutes | Serves: 4

Ingredients:

- Whole grain pizza dough (16 oz) (450g)
- Low-fat mozzarella cheese, shredded (1 cup) (100g)
- Fresh basil leaves (1/4 cup) (15g)
- Olive oil (1 tbsp) (15ml)
- Salt and pepper to taste
- Cherry tomatoes, sliced (1 cup) (150g)

Instructions:

1. Preheat oven to 475°F (245°C). Divide dough into 4 portions and roll out into mini pizza bases.
2. Place bases on a baking sheet lined with parchment paper.
3. Top each base with mozzarella, tomato slices, and a drizzle of olive oil. Season with salt, pepper.
4. Bake for 10 minutes, or until crust is golden and cheese is bubbly.
5. Garnish with fresh basil before serving.

Nutritional Facts (Per Serving): Calories: 450 | Sugars: 4g | Fat: 10g | Carbohydrates: 65g | Protein: 25g | Fiber: 10g | Sodium: 10g

Stuffed Peppers with Quinoa and Low-Fat Feta

Prep: 20 minutes | Cook: 30 minutes | Serves: 4

Ingredients:

- Bell peppers (4 large) (900g)
- Quinoa, cooked (1 cup) (170g)
- Low-fat feta cheese, crumbled (1/2 cup) (75g)
- Red onion, finely chopped (1/2 cup) (80g)
- Olive oil (1 tbsp) (15ml)
- Salt and pepper to taste
- Spinach, chopped (1 cup) (30g)

Instructions:

1. Preheat oven to 350°F (175°C).
2. Halve peppers lengthwise, removing seeds. Place in a baking dish.
3. In a bowl, mix quinoa, feta, spinach, onion, olive oil, salt, and pepper.
4. Stuff peppers with quinoa mixture. Cover with foil.
5. Bake for 30 minutes, until peppers are tender.
6. Serve warm.

Nutritional Facts (Per Serving): Calories: 450 | Sugars: 10g | Fat: 15g | Carbohydrates: 65g | Protein: 20g | Fiber: 10g | Sodium: 10g

Lemon-Herb Calamari Rings with Yogurt Dip

Prep: 15 minutes | Cook: 10 minutes | Serves: 2

Ingredients:

- 1 lb calamari rings (450g)
- 1/2 cup all-purpose flour (60g)
- 1 tsp paprika (2g)
- 1/2 tsp garlic powder (1g)
- Salt and pepper to taste
- 2 tbsp olive oil (30ml)
- Zest of 1 lemon
- 1 tbsp lemon juice (15ml)

For Yogurt Dip:
- 1/2 cup Greek yogurt (120g)
- 1 tbsp chopped fresh dill (3g)
- 1 tsp lemon zest
- 1 tbsp lemon juice (15ml)
- Salt and pepper to taste

Instructions:

1. In a bowl, combine flour, paprika, garlic powder, salt, and pepper.
2. Toss calamari rings in the flour mixture to coat evenly.
3. Heat olive oil in a skillet over medium heat. Add calamari rings and cook until golden and crisp, about 2-3 minutes per side.
4. In a small bowl, mix Greek yogurt, dill, lemon zest, lemon juice, salt, and pepper to make the dip.
5. Serve calamari rings with a sprinkle of lemon zest and lemon juice, alongside the yogurt dip.

Nutritional Facts (Per Serving): Calories: 370 | Sugars: 3g | Fat: 15g | Carbohydrates: 30g | Protein: 30g | Fiber: 1g | Sodium: 400m

Braised Cod with Olives and Capers

Prep: 10 minutes | Cook: 20 minutes | Serves: 4

Ingredients:

- Cod fillets (4) (600g total)
- Olive oil (1 tbsp) (15ml)
- Cherry tomatoes, halved (1 cup) (150g)
- Black olives, pitted (1/4 cup) (30g)
- Capers, rinsed (2 tbsp) (16g)
- Garlic, minced (2 cloves) (6g)
- Dry white wine (1/2 cup) (120ml)
- Fresh parsley, chopped (1/4 cup) (15g)
- Salt and pepper to taste

Instructions:

1. Heat olive oil in a large skillet over medium heat.
2. Add garlic and sauté until fragrant.
3. Add cod fillets, season with salt and pepper. Cook for 2 minutes on each side.
4. Add cherry tomatoes, olives, capers, and white wine. Cover and simmer for 15 minutes.
5. Garnish with fresh parsley before serving.

Nutritional Facts (Per Serving): Calories: 350 | Sugars: 2g | Fat: 10g | Carbohydrates: 5g | Protein: 50g | Fiber: 1g | Sodium: 5g

Seafood Paella with Saffron, More Seafood, Less Rice

Prep: 20 minutes | Cook: 30 minutes | Serves: 4

Ingredients:

- Short-grain rice (1 cup) (200g)
- Chicken broth (2 cups) (480ml)
- Saffron threads (a pinch)
- Olive oil (2 tbsp) (30ml)
- Mixed seafood (shrimp, mussels, clams) (1 lb) (450g total)
- Green peas (1/2 cup) (75g)
- Red bell pepper, sliced (1) (150g)
- Garlic, minced (1 clove) (3g)
- Salt and pepper to taste

Instructions:

1. Heat chicken broth and infuse with saffron.
2. Heat olive oil in a paella pan or large skillet. Sauté garlic and bell pepper.
3. Add rice, stirring to coat with oil. Pour in saffron-infused broth. Simmer for 10 minutes.
4. Add seafood and peas, cover, and cook until seafood is cooked through and rice is tender, about 20 minutes.
5. Let stand for 5 minutes before serving.

Nutritional Facts (Per Serving): Calories: 380 | Sugars: 3g | Fat: 10g | Carbohydrates: 40g | Protein: 30g | Fiber: 2g | Sodium: 5g

Risotto with Sea Scallops and Green Peas

Prep: 15 minutes | Cook: 25 minutes | Serves: 4

Ingredients:

- Arborio rice (1 cup) (200g)
- Chicken or vegetable broth (4 cups) (960ml)
- Sea scallops (1 lb) (450g)
- Green peas, frozen or fresh (1 cup) (150g)
- Olive oil (1 tbsp) (15ml)
- White wine (1/2 cup) (120ml)
- Parmesan cheese, grated (1/4 cup) (25g)
- Salt and pepper to taste

Instructions:

1. Heat broth in a separate pot.
2. Heat olive oil in a large skillet over medium heat.
3. Sear scallops until golden, set aside.
4. In the same skillet, add rice and stir for 2 minutes. Add wine and cook until absorbed.
5. Add broth 1/2 cup at a time, stirring constantly, until rice is creamy and al dente, about 18 minutes.
6. Stir in peas, cook for 2 minutes. Add scallops back to the skillet to warm through.
7. Stir in Parmesan, season with salt and pepper.

Nutritional Facts (Per Serving): Calories: 380 | Sugars: 3g | Fat: 10g | Carbohydrates: 45g | Protein: 30g | Fiber: 3g | Sodium: 5g

Grilled Dorado with Vegetables and Herbs, Light Dressing

Prep: 15 minutes | Cook: 20 minutes | Serves: 4

Ingredients:

- Dorado fillets (4) (600g total)
- Zucchini, sliced (1 medium) (200g)
- Bell peppers, sliced (2 medium) (300g)
- Olive oil (2 tbsp) (30ml)
- Lemon juice (2 tbsp) (30ml)
- Fresh herbs (basil, parsley) (1/4 cup) (15g)
- Salt and pepper to taste
- Cherry tomatoes (1 cup) (150g)

Instructions:

1. Preheat grill to medium-high heat.
2. Toss vegetables with 1 tablespoon olive oil, salt, and pepper. Grill until charred and tender, about 10 minutes.
3. Brush dorado fillets with remaining olive oil and season with salt and pepper. Grill for about 3-4 minutes on each side.
4. Whisk together lemon juice, chopped herbs, and a pinch of salt for the dressing.
5. Serve grilled dorado with vegetables, drizzled with herb-lemon dressing.

Nutritional Facts (Per Serving): Calories: 350 | Sugars: 4g | Fat: 12g | Carbohydrates: 20g | Protein: 40g | Fiber: 5g | Sodium: 5g

Sea Bass in Foil with Lemon and Rosemary, No Butter

Prep: 10 minutes | Cook: 15 minutes | Serves: 4

Ingredients:

- Sea bass fillets (4) (600g total)
- Lemon, thinly sliced (1)
- Fresh rosemary sprigs (4)
- Olive oil (1 tbsp) (15ml)
- Salt and pepper to taste

Instructions:

1. Preheat oven to 400°F (200°C).
2. Cut 4 sheets of foil, large enough to wrap each fillet.
3. Place a fillet on each foil, top with lemon slices, a sprig of rosemary, drizzle with olive oil, and season with salt and pepper.
4. Fold the foil over the fish, sealing the edges to create a packet.
5. Bake for 15 minutes, or until fish is cooked through.
6. Carefully open packets and serve immediately.

Nutritional Facts (Per Serving): Calories: 360 | Sugars: 0g | Fat: 10g | Carbohydrates: 0g | Protein: 60g | Fiber: 0g | Sodium: 5g

Squid Stuffed with Vegetables and Wild Rice

Prep: 30 minutes | Cook: 20 minutes | Serves: 4

Ingredients:

- Large squid, bodies cleaned (4) (600g)
- Wild rice, cooked (1 cup) (165g)
- Zucchini, finely chopped (1/2 cup) (100g)
- Red bell pepper, finely chopped (1/2 cup) (75g)
- Onion, finely chopped (1/4 cup) (40g)
- Garlic, minced (2 cloves) (6g)
- Olive oil (2 tbsp) (30ml)
- Tomato sauce (1/2 cup) (120ml)
- Salt and pepper to taste

Instructions:

1. Preheat oven to 375°F (190°C).
2. Sauté onion, garlic, zucchini, and bell pepper in 1 tablespoon olive oil until soft. Mix with wild rice, season with salt and pepper.
3. Stuff squid bodies with the rice mixture, secure ends with toothpicks.
4. Place stuffed squid in a baking dish, cover with tomato sauce and drizzle with remaining olive oil.
5. Bake for 20 minutes, or until squid is tender.
6. Serve warm.

Nutritional Facts (Per Serving): Calories: 380 | Sugars: 4g | Fat: 10g | Carbohydrates: 40g | Protein: 40g | Fiber: 5g | Sodium: 5g

Baked Mussels with Parmesan and Garlic

Prep: 15 minutes | Cook: 10 minutes | Serves: 4

Ingredients:

- Fresh mussels, cleaned (24) (960g)
- Garlic, minced (4 cloves) (12g)
- Parmesan cheese, grated (1/2 cup) (50g)
- Fresh parsley, chopped (1/4 cup) (15g)
- Olive oil (2 tbsp) (30ml)
- Breadcrumbs (1/4 cup) (30g)
- Lemon wedges (for serving)
- Salt and pepper to taste

Instructions:

1. Preheat oven to 400°F (200°C). Arrange mussels on a baking sheet.
2. In a bowl, mix garlic, Parmesan, parsley, breadcrumbs, olive oil, salt, and pepper.
3. Spoon mixture onto each mussel.
4. Bake for 10 minutes, or until breadcrumbs are golden and mussels have opened.
5. Serve with lemon wedges on the side.

Nutritional Facts (Per Serving): Calories: 350 | Sugars: 2g | Fat: 15g | Carbohydrates: 20g | Protein: 35g | Fiber: 1g | Sodium: 5g

Tuna Steak with Tomato Salsa

Prep: 20 minutes | Cook: 10 minutes | Serves: 4

Ingredients:

- Tuna steaks (4) (600g total)
- Cherry tomatoes, diced (1 cup) (150g)
- Red onion, finely chopped (1/4 cup) (40g)
- Cilantro, chopped (1/4 cup) (15g)
- Olive oil (for salsa) (1 tbsp) (15ml), (for tuna) (1 tbsp) (15ml)
- Lime juice (2 tbsp) (30ml)
- Salt and pepper to taste

Instructions:

1. Preheat grill to high heat.
2. For the salsa, combine tomatoes, onion, cilantro, 1 tbsp olive oil, lime juice, salt, and pepper in a bowl.
3. Brush tuna steaks with 1 tbsp olive oil and season with salt and pepper.
4. Grill tuna for about 3-4 minutes per side for medium-rare.
5. Serve tuna topped with tomato salsa.

Nutritional Facts (Per Serving): Calories: 380 | Sugars: 3g | Fat: 10g | Carbohydrates: 10g | Protein: 55g | Fiber: 2g | Sodium: 5g

Baked Mackerel with Lemon and Olives

Prep: 15 minutes | Cook: 20 minutes | Serves: 4

Ingredients:

- Mackerel fillets (4) (600g total)
- Lemons, thinly sliced (2)
- Olives, pitted (1/4 cup) (30g)
- Fresh rosemary (1 tbsp) (1g)
- Olive oil (2 tbsp) (30ml)
- Salt and pepper to taste

Instructions:

1. Preheat oven to 375°F (190°C).
2. Arrange lemon slices on a baking dish and place mackerel fillets on top. Season with salt and pepper.
3. Scatter olives and rosemary over the fillets. Drizzle with olive oil.
4. Bake for 20 minutes, or until mackerel is cooked through.
5. Serve immediately.

Nutritional Facts (Per Serving): Calories: 350 | Sugars: 0g | Fat: 20g | Carbohydrates: 5g | Protein: 35g | Fiber: 2g | Sodium: 5g

Shrimp with Grilled Vegetables and Citrus Sauce, More Veggies

Prep: 20 minutes | Cook: 15 minutes | Serves: 4

Ingredients:

- Shrimp, peeled and deveined (1 lb) (450g)
- Zucchini, sliced (2 medium) (400g)
- Bell peppers, sliced (2 medium) (300g)
- Asparagus, trimmed (1 cup) (135g)
- Olive oil (2 tbsp) (30ml)
- Salt and pepper to taste

For the Citrus Sauce:
- Orange juice (1/4 cup) (60ml),
- Lemon juice (2 tbsp) (30ml),
- Olive oil (1 tbsp) (15ml),
- Honey (1 tsp) (5ml),
- Garlic, minced (1 clove) (3g)

Instructions:

1. Preheat grill to medium-high heat.
2. Toss vegetables with 1 tablespoon olive oil, salt, and pepper. Grill until tender and charred, about 10 minutes.
3. Toss shrimp with remaining olive oil and season with salt and pepper. Grill until pink and opaque, about 2-3 minutes per side.
4. For the citrus sauce, whisk together orange juice, lemon juice, olive oil, honey, and minced garlic.
5. Serve grilled shrimp and vegetables drizzled with citrus sauce.

Nutritional Facts (Per Serving): Calories: 350 | Sugars: 5g | Fat: 12g | Carbohydrates: 20g | Protein: 40g | Fiber: 5g | Sodium: 5g

Fish Patties with Herbs and Lemon Aioli

Prep: 25 minutes | Cook: 10 minutes | Serves: 4

Ingredients:

- White fish fillets (1 lb) (450g), cooked and flaked
- Fresh herbs (parsley, dill) (1/4 cup) (15g)
- Bread crumbs (1/2 cup) (60g)
- Olive oil for frying (2 tbsp) (30ml)

- Egg (1 large)
- Salt and pepper to taste

For Lemon Aioli:
- Low-fat greek yogurt (1/2 cup) (120ml),
- Lemon zest (1 tsp) (2g)
- Lemon juice (1 tbsp) (15ml)
- Garlic, minced (1 clove) (3g)

Instructions:

1. In a bowl, combine flaked fish, herbs, bread crumbs, egg, salt, and pepper. Form into patties.
2. Heat olive oil in a pan over medium heat. Cook patties until golden, about 5 minutes per side.
3. For lemon aioli, mix Greek yogurt, lemon zest, lemon juice, and garlic.
4. Serve fish patties with a dollop of lemon aioli.

Nutritional Facts (Per Serving): Calories: 380 | Sugars: 2g | Fat: 20g | Carbohydrates: 20g | Protein: 35g | Fiber: 2g | Sodium: 5g

Branzino with Tomatoes and Capers in White Wine, Light Sauce

Prep: 15 minutes | Cook: 20 minutes | Serves: 4

Ingredients:

- Bronzino fillets (4) (600g)
- Cherry tomatoes, halved (1 cup) (150g)
- Capers (2 tbsp) (16g)
- White wine (1/2 cup) (120ml)

- Olive oil (2 tbsp) (30ml)
- Garlic, minced (2 cloves) (6g)
- Fresh parsley, chopped (1/4 cup) (15g)
- Salt and pepper to taste

Instructions:

1. Preheat oven to 375°F (190°C).
2. In a baking dish, arrange Bronzino fillets. Scatter tomatoes, capers, and garlic around the fish.
3. Drizzle with olive oil and white wine. Season with salt and pepper.
4. Bake for 20 minutes, until fish is cooked through.
5. Garnish with fresh parsley before serving.

Nutritional Facts (Per Serving): Calories: 350 | Sugars: 3g | Fat: 12g | Carbohydrates: 5g | Protein: 50g | Fiber: 1g | Sodium: 5g

Braised Perch with Vegetables in Tomato Sauce

Prep: 15 minutes | Cook: 30 minutes | Serves: 4

Ingredients:

- Perch fillets (4) (600g)
- Zucchini, sliced (1 medium) (200g)
- Carrots, sliced (2 medium) (150g)
- Onion, chopped (1 medium) (100g)
- Canned diced tomatoes (2 cups) (480ml)
- Olive oil (1 tbsp) (15ml)
- Fresh basil, chopped (1/4 cup) (15g)
- Salt and pepper to taste
- Garlic, minced (2 cloves) (6g)

Instructions:

1. Heat olive oil in a large skillet over medium heat.
2. Sauté onion, garlic, carrots, and zucchini until softened, about 5 minutes.
3. Add diced tomatoes and bring to a simmer.
4. Season perch fillets with salt and pepper, then nestle them into the skillet with the vegetables.
5. Cover and simmer gently for 20 minutes, or until fish is cooked through.
6. Garnish with fresh basil before serving.

Nutritional Facts (Per Serving): Calories: 350 | Sugars: 5g | Fat: 10g | Carbohydrates: 20g | Protein: 45g | Fiber: 5g | Sodium: 5g

Pasta with Shrimp and Garlic Sauce, Whole Wheat, Light on Oil

Prep: 10 minutes | Cook: 15 minutes | Serves: 4

Ingredients:

- Whole wheat pasta (8 oz) (225g)
- Shrimp, peeled and detained (1 lb) (450g)
- Garlic, minced (4 cloves) (12g)
- Olive oil (2 tbsp) (30ml)
- Red pepper flakes (1/2 tsp) (1g)
- Lemon juice (2 tbsp) (30ml)
- Fresh parsley, chopped (1/4 cup) (15g)
- Salt and pepper to taste

Instructions:

1. Cook pasta according to package instructions. Drain and set aside.
2. Heat olive oil in a large skillet over medium heat.
3. Add garlic and red pepper flakes, cooking until fragrant.
4. Add shrimp, season with salt and pepper, and cook until pink and opaque, about 2-3 minutes per side.
5. Toss cooked pasta and shrimp together with lemon juice and parsley.
6. Serve immediately.

Nutritional Facts (Per Serving): Calories: 380 | Sugars: 3g | Fat: 10g | Carbohydrates: 45g | Protein: 35g | Fiber: 7g | Sodium: 5g

CHAPTER 19: BONUSES

Meal Plans and Shopping Templates: Ready-to-use templates to simplify meal planning.

To enhance your Mediterranean diet experience, we've designed a 30-day grocery shopping guide, tailored to our cookbook. This guide simplifies meal prep, focusing on fresh, natural ingredients and minimizing processed foods. Be mindful of hidden sugars, especially in sauces and dressings. Adjust quantities to your needs, embracing the Mediterranean emphasis on whole foods. Enjoy the journey of healthy, flavorful cooking!

Grocery Shopping List for 7-Day Meal Plan

Proteins

Eggs (for Shakshuka with Tomatoes, Greek Yogurt with Honey and Nuts)
Ground Beef (for Greek Moussaka with Beef and Eggplant)
Chicken Breast (for Chicken and Spinach Lasagna, Chicken Bolognese Pasta with Basil)
Tuna Steaks (for Niçoise Salad with Grilled Tuna)
Salmon Fillets (for Baked Salmon with Thyme and Lemon)
Lamb (for Lamb Pilaf with Tomatoes)

Dairy and Dairy Alternatives:

Greek Yogurt (for Greek Yogurt with Honey and Nuts, Baked Sweet Potato Chips with Greek Yogurt)
Cottage Cheese (for Cottage Cheese Bake with Berries and Nuts)
Heavy Cream (for Panna Cotta with Lavender Syrup, Polenta with Mushrooms and Parmesan)
Low-Fat Feta Cheese (for Stuffed Peppers with Quinoa and Low-Fat Feta)
Parmesan Cheese (for Polenta with Mushrooms and Parmesan)
Butter (for various dishes)

Fruits:

Tomatoes (for Shakshuka, Pasta with Roasted Tomato and Basil Sauce, Mediterranean Fish Soup)
Figs (for Fresh Figs with Goat Cheese and Honey, Pie with Figs and Almonds)
Lemons (for Baked Salmon with Thyme and Lemon)
Mixed Berries (for Cottage Cheese Bake with Berries and Nuts)
Avocado (for Protein Smoothie with Spinach and Avocado)

Vegetables & Herbs:

Spinach (for Omelette with Feta and Spinach, Chicken and Spinach Lasagna)
Eggplant (for Greek Moussaka with Beef and Eggplant)
Broccoli (for Orecchiette with Broccoli, Garlic, and Olive Oil)
Bell Peppers (for Ratatouille, Stuffed Peppers with Quinoa and Low-Fat Feta)
Mushrooms (for Polenta with Mushrooms and Parmesan)
Garlic, Onions (for multiple dishes)
Fresh Herbs (basil, dill, parsley, thyme, etc.)

Grains & Bakery:

Whole Wheat Pasta (for Pasta dishes)
Couscous (for Couscous with Vegetables and Green Onions)
Polenta (for Polenta with Mushrooms and Parmesan)
Whole Grain Flour (for Whole Grain Pancakes with Fruit Sauce)

Nuts & Seeds:

Nuts (for Greek Yogurt with Honey and Nuts, Cottage Cheese Bake with Berries and Nuts)
Pine Nuts (for Niçoise Salad with Grilled Tuna)
Sesame Seeds (for Nut Halva with Honey and Sesame)
Almonds (for Pie with Figs and Almonds)

Pantry Staples:

Olive Oil (for various dishes)
Balsamic Vinegar (for Mediterranean Roasted Vegetable Salad)
Various Spices (cumin, paprika, pepper, etc.)
Honey (for various dishes)
Canned Tomatoes (for Shakshuka, Pasta Sauce)

Miscellaneous:

Gelatin (for Panna Cotta)
Cocoa Powder (for Low-Sugar Tiramisu with Whole Grain Biscuits)
Lavender (for Panna Cotta with Lavender Syrup)
Baking Ingredients (baking powder, vanilla extract, etc.)

Grocery Shopping List for 8-14 Day Meal Plan

Proteins

Chicken (for Braised Chicken with Olives, Lemon, and

Roasted Vegetables; Chicken Kebab with Yogurt Marinade)
Lamb (for Turkish Lamb Kebabs)
Beef (for Beef Meatballs, Beef Stew)
Mackerel (for Baked Mackerel with Lemon and Olives)
Cod (for Braised Cod with Olives and Capers)
Sea Scallops (for Risotto with Sea Scallops)
Dorado Fish (for Grilled Dorado)

Dairy and Dairy Alternatives:

Low-Fat Mozzarella Cheese (for Mini Pizza)
Brie Cheese (for Tartlets)
Greek Yogurt (for Chicken Kebab Marinade, Fruit Salad with Mint and Yogurt)
Butter (for cooking and baking)

Fruits:

Avocado (for Quinoa Salad, Avocado and Orange Citrus Salad)
Oranges (for Avocado and Orange Citrus Salad)
Lemons (for Braised Chicken, Baked Mackerel, Dorado)
Figs (for Waffles)
Bananas (for Chocolate-Banana Pancakes)
Mixed Seasonal Fruits (for Muesli and Fruit Salad)

Vegetables & Herbs:

Spinach (for Lentil Soup, Beef Stew)
Mixed Vegetables (for Turkish Menemen, Beef Stew)

Onions, Garlic (for various dishes)
Broccoli (for Beef Meatballs)
Celery, Carrots (for Braised Pork)
Tomatoes (for Focaccia, Mini Pizza, Herbed Tomato Sauce)
Eggplant (for Eggplant Rolls)
Green Peas (for Risotto)
Fresh Herbs (mint, parsley, basil, thyme, etc.)

Grains & Bakery:

Quinoa (for Quinoa Salad)
Whole Grain Flour (for Mini Pizza, Focaccia)
Phyllo Dough (for Orange Phyllo Tartlets)
Whole Grain Bread (for Olive Tapenade)

Nuts & Seeds:

Nuts (for Muesli, Fruit Salad)

Pantry Staples:

Olive Oil (for various dishes)
Lentils (for Lentil Soup)
Tahini (for Falafel Sauce)
Honey (for Orange Phyllo Tartlets, Yogurt Popsicles)
Canned Tomatoes (for Meatballs Sauce, Ratatouille)
Baking Ingredients (sugar, baking powder, vanilla extract, etc.)
Capers (for Braised Cod)
Saffron (for Seafood Paella)

Miscellaneous:

Cocoa Powder (for Chocolate-Banana Pancakes)
Dark Chocolate (for Olive Oil Cake)

Seafood (shrimp, mussels, or others for Seafood Paella)
Gelatin (for Yogurt Popsicles)
Yogurt (for Yogurt Popsicles)

Frozen/Cold:

Frozen Mixed Berries (for Yogurt Popsicles)

Grocery Shopping List for 15-21 Day Meal Plan

Proteins:

Chicken Breast (for Chicken Rollatini, Grilled Chicken)
Sea Bass (for Sea Bass in Foil)
Squid (for Stuffed Squid)
Lamb (for Lamb Patties, Lamb Ribs)
Beef (for Beef Goulash)
Tuna Steaks (for Tuna Steak with Tomato Salsa)
Fish Fillets (for Fish Patties)

Dairy and Dairy Alternatives:

Mozzarella Cheese (for Caprese Salad)
Feta Cheese (for Chicken Rollatini, Omelette)
Parmesan Cheese (for Baked Mussels)
Ricotta Cheese (for Ricotta Cream with Berries)
Heavy Cream (for Panna Cotta)

Fruits:

Mixed Berries (for Fresh Berry Sorbet, Kefir Smoothie, Ricotta Cream)

Lemons (for Sea Bass, Grilled Chicken, Fish Patties)
Apples (for Apple Charlotte)
Avocado (for Poached Eggs with Salad)
Mango (for Mango and Coconut Milk Mousse)

Vegetables & Herbs:

Tomatoes (for Caprese Salad, Ciabatta, Branzi- no, Goulash)
Spinach (for Chicken Rollatini, Omelette)
Roasted Red Peppers (for Chicken Rollatini)
Asparagus (for Grilled Chicken)
Pumpkin (for Pumpkin Pancakes)
Zucchini (for Lamb Ribs)
Green Beans (for Beef Goulash)
Mixed Vegetables (for Squid Stuffing, Mediterranean Vegetables)
Artichokes (for Chicken with Artichokes)
Basil, Rosemary, Mint, and other fresh herbs

Grains & Bakery:

Whole Grain Flour (for Pancakes)
Ciabatta Bread (for Ciabatta with Tomatoes)
Couscous (for Couscous with Vegetables)
Wild Rice (for Squid Stuffed with Vegetables)

Nuts & Seeds:

Nuts (for Pumpkin Pancakes, Almond Cookies)
Almond Flour (for Almond Cookies)

Pantry Staples:

Olive Oil (for various dishes)
Honey (for Pancakes, Ricotta Cream)
Canned Tomatoes (for Goulash, Branzi- no)
Coconut Milk (for Mango Mousse)
Wine (for Chicken with Wine Sauce)
Capers (for Baked Mussels, Branzi- no)

Miscellaneous:

Gelatin (for Panna Cotta)
Cocoa Powder (for Chocolate Mousse)
Baking Ingredients (baking powder, vanilla extract.)
Greek Yogurt (for Kefir Smoothie)
Kefir (for Kefir Smoothie)

Frozen/Cold:

Frozen Squid (if not fresh)

Grocery Shopping List for 22-28 Day Meal Plan

Proteins:

Beef (for Beef Vegetable Ragout)
Shrimp (for Pasta with Shrimp and Garlic Sauce)
Chicken Breast (for Grilled Chicken Fillet)
Pork (for Pork in Honey-Mustard Marinade)
Salmon (for Baked Salmon)

Eggs (for Scrambled Eggs, Poached Eggs)

Dairy and Dairy Alternatives:

Low-Fat Feta Cheese (for Stuffed Peppers, Marinated Feta)
Greek Yogurt (for Greek Yogurt with Honey and Nuts, Fruit Salad)
Brie Cheese (for Tartlets)
Milk (for Pancakes, Smoothie)

Fruits:

Mixed Berries (for Whole Grain Pancakes, Lemon Curd, Kefir Smoothie)
Lemons (for Lemon Curd, Braised Chicken)
Bananas (for Chocolate-Banana Pancakes)
Avocado (for Poached Eggs, Whole Grain Crackers with Salsa)
Seasonal Fruits (for Fruit Salad)

Vegetables & Herbs:

Artichokes (for Scrambled Eggs)

Olives (for Scrambled Eggs, Braised Chicken)
Tomatoes (for Grilled Chicken Fillet, Mediterranean Fish Soup, Gazpacho)
Cucumbers (for Tomato-Cucumber Salad, Gazpacho)
Eggplant (for Pork Marinade, Eggplant Caviar)
Green Salad Ingredients (lettuce, spinach, etc.)
Sweet Peppers (for Gazpacho)
Fresh Herbs (mint, dill, basil, parsley, rosemary, etc.)

Grains & Bakery:

Whole Grain Flour (for Pancakes)
Whole Wheat Pasta (for Pasta with Shrimp, Pasta Primavera, Orecchiette)
Quinoa (for Quinoa Salad, Stuffed Peppers)
Whole Grain Crackers (for Avocado and Tomato Salsa)

Nuts & Seeds:

Nuts (for Greek Yogurt with Honey and Nuts)

Pantry Staples:

Olive Oil (for various dishes)
Honey (for Greek Yogurt, Pork Marinade)
Mustard (for Pork Marinade)
Canned Tomatoes (for Fish Soup, Braised Perch)
Vegetable or Chicken Broth (for Soup, Ragout)
Balsamic Vinegar (for Tartlets)
Garlic, Onions (for multiple dishes)
Spices (paprika, curry powder, etc.)

Miscellaneous:

Kefir (for Kefir Smoothie)
Baking Ingredients (sugar, baking powder, vanilla extract, etc.)
Cocoa Powder (for Chocolate-Banana Pancakes)
Phyllo Dough (for Tartlets)

Frozen/Cold:

Frozen Peas (for Pasta Primavera)

Made in United States
Troutdale, OR
05/01/2024